LEOPARDS
at My Door

LEOPARDS
at My Door

PEACE CORPS, TANZANIA
1966-1967

HARRIET DENISON

A PEACE CORPS WRITERS BOOK

PEACE CORPS WRITERS
OAKLAND, CALIFORNIA

Leopards at My Door
Peace Corps, Tanzania, 1966-1967
ISBN 978-1-935925-42-2

Copyright ©2014 by Harriet Denison

An Imprint of Peace Corps Worldwide

For more information, contact peacecorpsworld-wide@gmail.com. Peace Corps Writers and the Peace Corps Writers colophon are trademarks of PeaceCorpsWorldwide.org.

Library of Congress Control Number: 2013955248

First Peace Corps Writers Edition, March, 2014

...But the New Frontier of which I speak
is not a set of promises. It is a
set of challenges....

The New Frontier is here
whether we seek it or not.

Beyond that frontier are
uncharted areas of science and space,
unsolved problems of peace and war,
unconquered problems of ignorance
and prejudice, unanswered questions
of poverty and surplus....

—JOHN F. KENNEDY
ACCEPTANCE SPEECH AT
DEMOCRATIC NATIONAL CONVENTION
JULY 15, 1960

Acknowledgments

During my two years in Mwanza, Tanzania, blue airmail letters were a lifeline to my family, recording my teaching activities at Bwiru Girls' Secondary School and my travels during school breaks. Reading the letters years later, I am flooded with memories.

My mother wrote to me at least once a week and I responded promptly out of habit. Some of my letters were dense with detail and excitement. Others included mundane narrations of day-to-day activities written to fill up the space. My parents shared them with my younger brother, Allen, a college student, and my older sister, Carol, a nurse in Portland, Oregon.

What is in the letters is true, but skeletal. Memories that flesh out the events are fickle, so I have been delighted to reconnect with some of my Peace Corps cohorts from that era to fill in gaps and attempt clarifications. With their permission, I have incorporated some of their recollections. Kay Puttock, Anita Foley, Kathy Simpson, and Winnie Goliday remembered school events that had escaped me. George Brose and I recalled details of Outward Bound training, wading through what we did then and how our rock climbing techniques developed later.

My current writing group in Portland, Oregon has been incredibly helpful with all of my writing for this book, especially the chapters on the Outward Bound, Climbing Mt. Kilimanjaro, and hitchhiking to Arusha. This has been a long project, and I have had different writer-helpers over the years, but Nancy LaPaglia and Katy Riker have been a part of this book from the beginning. Sandy Dorr edited the bulk of the text early in the process, and as always, her comments were insightful and constructive. Helena Lee, Ann Zawaski, Ruth Roth, and Shulamit Lotate proofread the first printing with amazing new eyes.

Maureen R. Michelson, who edited this latest version, has been patient and precise with this new author. Book designer Sherry Wachter, who designed the cover and the book interior, has been an agreeable and talented partner. My thanks go to everyone who contributed to this project.

HARRIET ON HER MT. KILIMANJARO CLIMB.

Contents

LEOPARDS
at My Door

CHAPTER ONE

Why the Peace Corps?

I was a high school senior when John F. Kennedy, Jr. became president. The only other president I knew was Dwight D. Eisenhower, a much older man and not a part of my life as a child. Kennedy was young, optimistic, and full of enthusiasm. When he said, "...the torch has been passed to a new generation," I knew he meant me.

President Kennedy promised an end to poverty and a permanent peace. No more threats of nuclear war. No more pictures of starving children. But he told us he could not do it alone. He invited *all* U.S. citizens to pitch in and get involved with the solution.

In President Kennedy's Inaugural Address on January 20, 1961, he said, "Ask not what your country can do for you—ask what you can do for your country."

I knew I would do just that when the time came.

Then President Kennedy set about getting it done. On March 1, 1961, he signed Executive Order 10924, which established formation of the Peace Corps. The first two groups of Peace Corps volunteers left for Ghana and Tanzania in August of that same year.

Neither of my parents completed college. "It was the Depression!" my father said. "My family didn't have the money."

My sister, Carol, my brother, Allen, and I knew it was important to our father that we get a good education, which included a college degree. Many times Pop said, "College is the key to your future." So, I always knew college was part of my life trajectory.

Choosing a college was left entirely up to me. I first heard about Pomona College in Claremont, California when the school's team won *College Bowl,* a television quiz show. During the show, they featured vignettes of the colleges competing in *College Bowl.* Pomona seemed like just what I wanted; small, liberal arts, and in Southern California. I liked chemistry, so on my college application, I put that as my tentative major.

When the acceptance came from Pomona College, it included an application for a scholarship. I knew we were neither poor nor rich, but that is all I could say about my family's finances at that time. I showed my father the college forms with many questions about the financial condition of our family. He took a quick look and blustered, "No, you don't need to fill that out. I'm not rich, but I'll find the money to pay for your education even if I end up in the poor house."

My father was prone to exaggeration, and I knew the poor house was not in his future. It did answer the scholarship question, but not much more. A short while later, my mother took me aside for a "little talk." She opened her family accounting book with green pages of vertical lines, company names down the left side and the squares meticulously filled with tiny numbers. She said, "Harriet, you will receive some money when you are older. Pop and I invested some for you when we were able and your grandmother left you some in her will. If you are very careful, you won't have to worry about money."

What does that mean to someone who has never lived outside the family? Be careful with money? She didn't have to mention that I should not be extravagant. My parents were married during the Depression, and habits acquired in their early years had imbued all of us children with a conservative attitude toward money. "Buy only what you need," they advised us. "Don't spend more than you have."

We learned what our allowances could and could not buy. We also learned what our parents would buy for us. They were not an easy touch.

Another remnant from their Depression years was a strong sense of community responsibility. My father told us that when he was a young man he hesitated to take the job his future father-in-law offered him because he felt other men, ones with families, needed it more. In addition, my parents were involved as volunteers in some capacity as I grew up and they set an example for us on how to give to others.

When President Kennedy said, as he often did, "To those whom much is given, much is expected," I felt he had singled me out of the crowd. I was eager to find what form that would take.

In the fall, I entered Pomona College, buoyed by the thrill of seeing so much movement within my country to make the world a safer and kinder place. While in college, I paid attention to the news as the Peace Corps sent more and more young people out into the world to wage peace.

I took the required courses for my major and my liberal arts degree. I wanted to travel, but a semester abroad was out of the question for a chemistry major. During my sophomore year, I read about the Pomona College partnership with Operation Crossroads Africa (OCA), a summer program for college students to work at the grassroots level with young Africans. The OCA worked in teams of ten to fifteen students on a community project in Africa. Five students from Pomona could participate. On their return, the students were required to give talks and speeches in the community to pass on what they learned and to raise money for the next OCA participants.

The civil rights movement was gaining momentum. I sympathized but did not really understand the issues, coming from Oregon, a very white state. All Crossroads' groups were well-integrated and included black and white college students from the United States, as well as from Canada.

What a grand opportunity, I thought. *And what more exciting place to spend a summer than Africa! Plus, what a great way to try out something like the Peace Corps.*

Later, I learned that James H. Robinson, Ph.D., a Presbyterian pastor at Harlem's Morningside Church in New York City, founded Crossroads in 1958. Dr. Robinson also served on the Peace Corps advisory board.

President Kennedy was assassinated in November 1963 and a profound grief settled over the country and the world. With a heavy heart, I applied for Crossroads Africa, determined to carry on Kennedy's dream. I was accepted for the 1964 program in Nyasaland, a British protectorate in Africa that was scheduled to become independent that summer. Soon after we arrived in Nyasaland, we attended the independence celebrations, and witnessed the birth of a new country, now officially called the Republic of Malawi.

The Africans were as stunned as we were at Kennedy's death. We were asked several times, "Why did you shoot him?" We had no answers.

My OCA group traveled on weekends, hung out in close quarters, and got to know each other well. The summer was rich with new experiences.

Our first leg home was a flight to Dar es Salaam, Tanzania. From there, a few of us took the ten-hour bus ride to Nairobi, the capital of Kenya. The unpaved road ran to the west of Mount Kilimanjaro. As the snowcapped mountain passed by my right shoulder and behind me, I already knew I would return.

During my senior year at Pomona, I focused on graduating, not an easy task. I was questioning the wisdom of my major, but by then, I just wanted to finish. President Lyndon B. Johnson was pushing progressive programs through Congress that President Kennedy had initiated. The number of Peace Corps Volunteers had grown and enthusiasm for the program was high among college students. While others made their post-graduation plans, such as medical school, graduate school, or internships, I wanted nothing more than to serve in the Peace Corps.

The aptitude test for the Peace Corps was administered on a Saturday morning. About thirty of us sat in a small classroom answering questions like, "Name as many uses for a bucket as you can," or "How many blocks are represented in the drawing below?" The drawing was a stack of blocks with staggered sides.

The test was a snap and I was accepted. On the form, I filled in the blank for my preferred assignment—East Africa, of course. My assignment would come later. Just before graduation, I was offered a position in Nigeria. I turned it down even though I knew I would not be able to do that too many times. My heart was set on East Africa.

Midsummer, the offer to teach sciences in a secondary school in Tanzania arrived. It was my dream assignment.

Most Peace Corps volunteers (PCVs) at that time were generalists, trained in community development. I heard they learned how to dig latrines and raise chickens. Then, they were told to take a bus ride for two days, walk two days, find a village, and do something good. However, many volunteers who went to Africa were teaching in primary and secondary schools. That felt like a better use of my skills, and suited me fine.

The previous summer when I went to Malawi with the Crossroads project, we had spent an afternoon with some Peace Corps teachers. They lived in regular houses and taught in towns with other volunteers. That seemed pretty cushy compared to some Peace Corps postings. I loved the idea of serving, but I did not really want to be the only person working on an isolated and amorphous project like so many Peace Corps volunteers were doing.

My group of Peace Corps volunteers was called Tanzania X, the tenth group to go to Tanzania. We trained for three months in the fall of 1965 at Syracuse University, learning Swahili, the history and culture of Tanzania, and general teaching skills. Student teaching in the local high schools gave us practical experience.

After spending Christmas with our families, we boarded a plane for Tanzania in January 1966. I felt ready to go and I was confident I had something to offer. We still had a few more days of orientation in Dar es Salaam before traveling to our schools. I was excited because soon I would be teaching!

The following are compilations of many letters I wrote to my family and recent conversations with friends who taught with me.

Harriet shopping in the market.

CHAPTER TWO

First School Term

SUNDAY, JANUARY 16, 1966

Dear Family,

Here at last! Steve Sterk, Winnie Golliday, and I climbed on to the train in Dar for our two-day trip with several others in our group. Peace Corps volunteers (PCVs) usually take second-class seats, but those seats were sold out, so Winnie I and traveled first class. The car was a bit newer and cleaner than the others were.

The English-style meals were fine, your basic meat and potatoes and overcooked veggies. Our little room had big windows to the outside, seats on the wall made into beds, and a sliding door to the passageway just like the trains Miss Marple takes in England. I opened up the window by lifting a limp leather strap at the bottom of the single frame. This pulled the heavy window out of a groove so I could lower it into the wall pocket. Clever, but we had to close it because the diesel smoke from the engine made us choke. Later, a little crosswind solved that problem.

The train chugged through the heart of Tanzania. Flat-topped acacia trees punctuated golden expanses of dried grasses and grey-green, spiny scrub brush. No wild animals approached the tracks, which seemed wise of them, though we could see a few antelope in the distance. Houses changed as we moved inland. The coastal mud-on-stick walls were round with peaked roofs; inland they became rectangular with flat roofs. As we approached Lake Victoria, the houses became round again, larger than on the coast.

On the train, one of the PCVs had his wallet stolen, so I lent him sixty shillings ($8.50). This left me with fewer than thirty shillings, which you will see was fortunate.

At stops along the way through Tanzania, we said goodbye to our friends, Fritz Snyder in Morogoro, Ingrid Samuelson and Went Fels in Dodoma, Diane DeLisle and Bernie Masterson in Tabora. Like us, they were destined to teach in secondary schools. We'd been together for almost four months training in Syracuse, New York. As they disappeared behind the train, I felt a twang of separation. Leaving them made this experience suddenly real.

The three of us still on the train arrived in Mwanza last Wednesday morning. Jack McPhee, the local Peace Corps representative, drove us the three miles out of town to our schools. A mile or so off the main road we dropped Steve at Bwiru Boys' Secondary School, and drove on to Bwiru Girls' Secondary School. The tradition of separating the genders seems to hold over from the British system. Until 1961, Tanganyika was a United Nations trust Territory administered by the United Kingdom, so the British influence was pervasive.

The Land Rover halted inside the entry gate to the girls' school. A well-dressed African woman approached and introduced herself as Mrs. Makonde, the headmistress of the school. A pleasant, chatty woman, she was clearly pleased that more teachers had arrived. Some call her Mama Mkubwa, big mother, which refers to her importance, not size, though she is a bit short and plump. Over tea at her house, she told us there were three Africans on the school staff. Most of the teachers were American, Canadian, and British. I was a little disappointed. I'd hoped to get to know some Tanzanian teachers, but we are training future teachers so I had to let that go.

Mrs. Makonde took us to the staff room and introduced us to the teachers who had returned from their school break. They were having their mid-morning tea in a room with a big table in the middle and more workspace built around the edges. In one corner, an electric kettle and teapot sat next to a plate of sweet biscuits. Winnie and I chatted briefly with the teachers over cups of tea, but I don't remember any names!

Mrs. Makonde called to a passing student who showed us the classrooms: adequate, but spare and dark. Nothing hung on the walls to brighten the rooms, no bookcases or shelves with interesting objects. Without students, the rooms felt rather bleak. I peeked in the large windows of the labs where I will teach. Those rooms looked bigger and brighter.

At lunch with Mrs. Makonde I was self-conscious, trying to please, impress, and chat all at once. Politely, I choked down a very spicy bite of tongue stew with rice and decided we'd better settle the housing quickly. You know tongue is my least favorite meat. The stew was so hot I needed a large portion of her rice. She noticed the tears streaming down my cheeks and diplomatically pushed the mango chutney in my direction. Hardly pausing in the conversation, she said, "It really cuts the heat."

Winnie and I had the choice of living together in a very distant house that Mrs. Makonde said was subject to burglaries, or sharing two already occupied and equipped houses that could each accommodate another person. It would have been fun to live with Winnie, but given the distance and danger of the first house, we chose to split up. One vacancy was with a British teacher, Kay, who is with TEA (Teachers for East Africa). She teaches English, and the other vacancy is with a PC volunteer who teaches "maths"—that's the British name for math. I couldn't remember much about the people I'd met that morning so, based on very little information, Winnie chose the math teacher, Shirley, and I took the other.

Living with Kay is a lucky choice because she is paid more than I am so she has dishes, cutlery, bookshelves, and a car, a VW bug. TEA teachers are American or British and are only secondary school teachers. The Peace Corps just began to send secondary school teachers, and no more Americans will be trained by TEA. Kay trained for a year in Uganda and while she is paid better, she doesn't have the in-country staff support we do. The previous PC programs were mostly primary school teachers in remote areas. Secondary schools draw students from a larger region and are located in towns that have more infrastructures. I don't think we need the support as much as they do. Politics must have played a part in replacing the TEA program with ours.

Our house is rectangular, made of cement blocks, and plastered and painted like most houses here. It has an open porch in the center with glass and metal French doors that lead to the living room. Two bedrooms and a bath are on one side with the kitchen and dining room on the other. It's surrounded and scented by poinsettia and frangipani, the same plant called plumeria, which I remember from our trip to Hawaii. A big bougainvillea with dark pink flowers grows up the blank face of the outer wall we pass coming home. From our porch a lovely path goes down to a lake. The soft sands and deep blue waves are tempting, but I'm resisting the bilharzia-infested water. No swimming for me!

Our Peace Corps orientation was held in Tanzania's biggest and richest city, Dar es Salaam, which means the "abode of peace." Most people shorten the name to "Dar" in conversations. During the conference, we learned about bilharzia, a most unpleasant disease that can be contracted in infested bodies of fresh water. (More on bilharzia later.) So, my last swim was in Dar, which has a salty bay that makes it safe from bilharzia. I succumbed to the challenge of diving off the channel marker since others were going off the thirty-foot tower. On the first dive, I learned that pointed hands just don't open a hole in the water. The top of my head hit hard. After that, I jumped.

Kay reads volumes and sometimes neglects her work, she says. She likes to cook. Fine by me since I don't. She seems to have a good sense of humor; she makes fun of stuffy Brits and says, "Oim Bratish" in a gargled voice. Then she laughs.

Juma, Kay's house "boy," cleans, does laundry, turns down our beds, and tucks in our mosquito nets before he goes home. Doing the net is fine, but I can do my own bed. It's a little strange to have someone else doing that. Kay says that with two people living in this house, we can afford to get a proper cook because Juma is a terrible cook, which is why Kay cooks a lot.

Anyway, classes started on Friday, mostly introductions and handing out books. I'm teaching only 20 hours a week. It's a light load, but I have Form III physics with chemistry, a combined course, which is mostly physics at this point. I also teach Forms I and II biology, even though I never took biology in college. I wanted to, but the pre-meds were so competitive. My high school class with Mr. Foulk will pull me through the biology courses. I have to do a lot of preparation, though. Drat! We have a written curriculum, so there's some direction. Physics just isn't my strength.

The labs where I teach are separate buildings the size of the house Kay and I live in with lots of windows. To teach and do demonstrations, I stand behind a twelve-foot-wide solid platform. The blackboard is behind me. The girls sit at tables used for experiments and lab work.

A form is like a high school year, so Form I is the same level as freshman year. We always use Form I, not Form One. Each form has 70 students in two sections, so I have four biology classes with 35 girls each. I am a little worried right now. I hope the training and student teaching we did in Syracuse was enough. Not much I can do about it now.

To get off to a good start, my wallet was stolen. There wasn't much money in it since I leant out most of it on the train. My passport is safe, but Mom, please send another copy of my birth certificate. Can you get me an international driver's license from triple A? Kay says I can drive her VW if I have a license. She only has a learner's permit, which means she should be driving with a licensed driver, but that doesn't stop her from driving alone. I think she is supposed to have a big "L" for learner on the car, like I see on other cars, so people know to stay out of her way.

Winnie and I shopped all day yesterday in Mwanza, a good-sized town of about 30,000 people. You can get anything you want of poor quality and no variety. There's one kind of toothpaste or soap. The men are dressed Western-style, a few in suits near the government offices. The shop owners in the commercial area had on white shirts and dark pants. The helpers' pants were a bit shiny from ironing with a too-hot iron. Many men not tending shops wear ratty T-shirts and khaki shorts; laborers and visiting villagers, I think.

The women usually wear a cotton dress with a *kanga,* a brightly patterned rectangle of cotton cloth wrapped around the waist. A second panel of the same pattern might be used to carry a baby on the woman's back or to wrap together a load that she balances on her head.

The local market is located near the center of town. It has a cement floor and a wide tin roof. Items for sale are displayed on cement benches. Vegetables, fruit, and eggs are in one section, meat in another. At the edges of the market are a few non-food vendors with small selections of children's clothes, plastic shoes, rope and hinges, and other things. We stepped across hoses and sloshed through puddles created by the people who were cleaning up. The vendors talk to each other in Swahili. Rather, they yell a lot because with all the activity it's quite noisy.

We bought a few things to try out our language skills, which are pretty basic. Winnie is Black and the people at the stalls couldn't believe she is an American, so they wouldn't acknowledge that. One man insisted on knowing Winnie's tribe, a traditional part of greeting someone in Tanzania. Without that information, he didn't seem to be able to understand what Winnie was saying even though her Swahili is good.

I can get the gist of what is being said, but I want to polish my Swahili so I can really understand what people are saying. Swahili is an ancient trade language created by the Arab traders, so it is no one's first language, a good thing with so many tribes in this area.

On the road home, we passed women carrying bundles of firewood, sugar cane, and maize stalks. Either the men pushed a loaded bike, or they peddled with a woman balanced on the back, legs sticking out to the side. We even saw one man with two children on the front bar as well. Every horizontal part of the bike frame can be a seat for someone. Boys with thin sticks beat the backs of cattle that moseyed along the side, stopping for a bite of grass when the mood moved them. Everywhere are the *kopjes,* huge natural formations of rocks that look like a giant child has piled them.

I feel overwhelmed and I'm scrambling to remember everything I've been told. This stage of my two-year tour is exciting and new, and at the same time frightening and a bit depressing. I'll be glad when I know what I'm doing.

Harriet

SUNDAY, JANUARY 22, 1966

Dear All,

All the teachers take turns doing "lights out," making sure the girls are present and in bed. Last Sunday, I decided to go with Shirley to learn what to do. Usually the lights go out at 9:30 p.m., but this week it's later due to Ramadan, the Muslim holy days that last for a month. The Muslim girls fast all day and can only eat after sunset, so they devour a good meal at 7 p.m. The cooks leave them snacks for 10 p.m. to eat before they go to bed, so they get two meals a day. The cooks don't come early enough for breakfast before school, so some girls get a bit groggy during classes. Someone said the most devout Moslems don't even swallow their spit in the daylight during Ramadan, but I haven't seen any of the girls spitting, so I guess they are a bit more liberal.

Shirley's house is about 100 yards from mine by way of the shortest route, a path overgrown with tall grass. I grabbed my powerful "torch" (flashlight) and left for her house at 10 p.m. I had been hearing some grunts outside our house, but thought they were hyenas. Everyone says they will run if they see you. Just in case, I traded the shortcut for a longer but wider, safer route, the one I take to school, past the frangipani border. As I stepped onto the car track toward Shirley's, I heard another grunt.

In the light of my torch, a figure jumped into the brush about twenty feet away. The slim spotted body moved like a cat. A leopard! I switched off my torch and ran to Shirley's. She was wide-eyed at my story. As I told it, I realized I had run right by the leopard. It must have been as startled as I was. Maybe my rattled brain figured it was running away too fast to turn and eat me.

That night, we decided to skip our dormitory duty. We had tea and peeked out the windows for an hour, but never saw the leopard again. Shirley invited me to sleep on her couch, which I thought was a fine idea.

When her cook arrived in the morning, he told us he'd seen the leopard at dawn. We found a paw print four inches across in the dust, not very big according to the cook but big enough for me. Even though Mwanza is only a few miles up the road, we are in a rural area and close to the Serengeti. People live in the valleys but the rocky ridges in between are thickly covered with prickly bushes and a few scrubby trees—perfect leopard habitat. During the day, we can hear the whistling of the rock hyraxes, tasty tidbits for a leopard. Hyraxes are cat-sized, piggy-shaped mammals with pointy noses.

A few things would make life easier. My window screens need replacing, the tub takes an hour to drain, and the toilet overflowed. My tape recorder only plays for an hour before it dies and I have to recharge the battery.

A couple of nights ago I took my first "prep" duty to monitor the students studying in their classrooms. The girls were quiet, so I watched a bat flit around in the staff room. They live in the rafters and as the light fades, they get restless, preparing to hunt. When the action started, I waited outside and watched the eaves until I saw a squinty little bat face poking out from under the grass roofing. If I flashed my torch on it, it disappeared for a moment. I'm easily entertained but impatient; the bat didn't have to wait long for me to leave.

Wow, last night the rain was just pelting until about 8:30. This morning more rain threatened. The ground was wet and muddy, so I wore my poncho and boots when I left the house. Approaching the classrooms, I saw the girls standing in little clusters and whispering to each other behind their hands, pointing at me with their chins, giggling, and turning away. During my class, I let one of them wear the poncho to get a new book from another building. She did so gladly. They will all be wearing ponchos soon, I'm sure.

Kay is still trying to train Juma to her standards of service. This morning, she said to me, "Imagine, Juma put jam out for breakfast instead of marmalade." Good thing I didn't set the table. She'd be furious at me.

Last night, a bunch of us went to see *Tom Jones*. The film didn't arrive, which apparently is common, so we watched an East Indian cowboys-and-Indians flick. Upper primary PCVs live in pretty remote areas. One couple had driven 60 miles to see the movie. They used the trip to visit friends, do some shopping, and have a restaurant meal, so it wasn't a total loss. I am sure lucky to live so close to town.

Harriet

SUNDAY, FEBRUARY 13, 1966

Dear Carol and Everyone,

What a nice surprise to get your card right on my birthday because our mail comes at strange times. Diane, a TEA like Kay, delivered it last Sunday on her way back from church.

Shirley invited Kay and me to dinner with her and Winnie. It was quite a nice gathering, which opens the way for thumbnail sketches of a few people here.

Mrs. Berry is a dignified, fifty-plus British teacher, well respected, not at all stuffy. I don't know what happened to her husband. She is our wise woman. The younger teachers chat with her about personal issues on occasion. Mrs. Makonde consults with her on administrative things because she has so much experience. Mrs. Berry will retire to England in May. Her hips bother her from an old horseback riding accident she had in Bechuanaland, Africa. She uses a cane and is quite heavy. I'm sure she was more mobile before her accident. She's lived in Africa for most of her life.

Betty and Dave Merchant are PCVs. Dave taught in middle schools until they got married last August. Dave has been in Tanzania three years and extended his stay to be with Betty. He is the only man on the staff. They have two dogs. Dogger is a small mongrel. Sam eats bones and is kind of like a pit bull, chunky with short legs, but not at all ferocious.

Phyllis is one for the books! She is one of the last American TEAs and almost finished with her service. She took Winnie to the Serengeti in her car and didn't take any money with her. Winnie had to pay for the gas, entrance fees, etc. When the weather turned bad, they returned early. Phyllis screwed up the calculations and figured Winnie owed her money and then tried to get Winnie to buy all the surplus food! She is not very popular here and leaves in May.

Winnie lives with Shirley, another Peace Corps volunteer. Shirley has been upset with Winnie recently. Winnie admits to not being a good roommate. Shirley, whose confessed primary fault is indecision, finally had to speak up. She asked Winnie if she wouldn't like to move into Phyllis's house when she leaves, a rather oblique solution in my opinion. Now, Shirley wants me to live with her. I'll think about it, but Kay and I get along well enough, and I might go nuts with Shirley. No matter what she asks you, when you answer, she says "Well, do you really think...." Or she'll ask your opinion then, and ask if you really think so. Every time.

Harriet

TUESDAY, FEBRUARY 15, 1966

Dear Carol,

I just wrote, but this time I have to thank you for the work on the international driver's license, which I look forward to receiving soon. I mailed some slides of the school to you, some taken from a nearby hill that show the layout. The school property is referred to as a compound, though many compounds have a fence or wall around them. We are at the end of a peninsula with Lake Victoria on three sides. A rocky slope separates us from the rest of the peninsula. It's not impassable, but not very convenient either for clandestine access by suitors, although apparently, thieves don't have any problems.

The school buildings are scattered along the shore and up away from the lake. Three staff houses are quite close to the lake. Ours is in the middle, Mrs. Berry's is on one side, and Dave and Betty Merchant's on the other side. In the morning, I walk from my house inland past the field where the girls muster around the flagpole and hear the announcements. To open, they sing the national anthem and harmonize beautifully. I'll sing it for you next time I see you, but it won't be the same with just one person singing.

Several of the slides I sent are of birds. I took a series of the weaver birds making their nests. Clever little guys. They start with a vertical circle made of grass and fill in the sides so it looks like a slightly elongated ball hanging down. They leave a hole in the bottom for the entrance. I think there must be some kind of partition inside or the eggs would fall out. The best trees for nests are covered with them! The birds are very chatty, happy with their colony. No leopard photos though. They just come around at night.

I got a letter from Mom today and in answer to her questions: even though there's lots of dirt around here, everyone is quite clean. The girls have showers, and the villagers can use the lake. The girls must wear uniforms, white cotton blouses and pastel green skirts during school hours, but can wear what they want otherwise. Often, it's a *kanga* with a blouse. They all do their laundry on the weekend in the washing troughs outside the bathhouses. I've seen them ironing with charcoal irons, so there may be some sort of inspection. When I do lights out, I often see the irons smoldering outside. An article in the paper the other day documented a whole family that died because they left a warm charcoal iron inside their

house when they went to bed. They all suffocated—
sad, but not uncommon.

Yes, we have a refrigerator, fueled by propane. It
sits in the dining room because the propane stove,
sink, prep table, and a stand for the water filter fill the
tiny kitchen.

Bilharzia infects many people in this area. We took
a group from school to the Bilharzia Research Center
in town, which will close soon. Lack of money. The
way they infect research animals is just horrid. We
watched while a researcher dropped a guinea pig into
a beaker of water full of the schistosomes (invisible)
that cause the disease. It was large enough so the
guinea pig could stand up on his tiptoes and reach the
top, but a glass plate held him inside. He was chewing
and scratching and so panicky I felt awful for him. The
researcher said he leaves him in there for an hour to
make sure he is infected.

After doing major damage to the mammalian host—
the guinea pig or people—the schistosomes lay their
eggs, which are "dispersed," i.e., they leave the host in
the poop. Most rural people do not use toilets, but do
their business at the side of a stream or lake so they can
clean themselves with the water afterward. The poop
washes into the lake, the eggs hatch, and the schistosomes infect a specific variety of snail, which is abundant here. They hang out in the snails. In the next stage,
they leave the snail to find people again. Cycle complete.

Schistosomes in the lake burrow into people. They go
right through your skin and cause a rash, sometimes
called swimmers' itch. I think other things can cause
the itch as well. Because schistosomes slice up livers,
kidneys, and other organs as they wander around the
host, my image of them is tiny swimming razor blades.

People who are heavily infected pee blood. It's one of
those things that is hard to diagnose because the person

is just very weak. Several of the girls suffer from bilharzia, also called schistosomiasis. It's tough for a student because we have our share of malingerers. The student has to convince the nurse she really is sick. There is no cure in spite of the efforts of the research center. Right now, the best they can do is to give some vile medicine with aluminum in it. If it doesn't kill you, it might kill the schistosomes. While research on a cure continues, one solution is to convince people to use proper pit toilets, which would keep the poop from the water.

By the way, our water does come from the lake, through a pump house beyond the last building. I hope the intake is out beyond the snails. The lake water is stored in a small tank in our attic and sits long enough for the schistosomes, if there are any, to die. I guess the bath water is safe because I've never felt itchy. Juma boils and filters all our drinking water. It goes through two porous cones in the top half of a ceramic tank and drips into the bottom part. You have to wash off the cones weekly because fuzzy brown stuff grows on them.

A local man brings our milk to the kitchen door in a quart-sized brown beer bottle with a twist of corn leaf for a stopper. Juma boils that as well. When it cools, a thick skin of cream forms on top. It's *nummy*, especially on smashed bananas.

Kay has a small black and white cat. We can't tell if it is a male or female, but I think it's pregnant. Maybe it just has worms because its stomach is huge. It whines wretchedly when it's hungry.

If you are thinking of visiting, our last day of school in 1966 is November 23. We begin again in the middle of January. December is supposed to be the short rainy season, but right now the season's rains have just begun. It's no worse than Oregon rain, but a bigger problem because most of the roads here are unpaved, and the mud can get pretty deep. If you are thinking of flying in or out, you should know that the airstrip is close to the lake and sometimes goes partly underwater.

The golf course is also on the lake, and one of the golfers told me that there is a special rule: If your ball lands in a hippo footprint you can take it out without a penalty. It was even in *Ripley's Believe It or Not*. I wonder what the planes do. The temperature is in the 70s, which is close to ideal for me.

I bought a bicycle for 395 shillings, about $56. The Peace Corps will reimburse me for 300 shillings if I ever fill out the form. Last Saturday, Shirley and I rode our bicycles to town and back. It was fun going in, half downhill and half flat. We planned to stop on our return trip at the McPhee's house, the Peace Corps rep. They live part way up our hill. We were going to just "pop in" for a glass of water to get us to the school, but no one was home. Oh, well.

Mrs. Berry and Dave had birthdays last Saturday the 12th. I gave Mrs. Berry a lei I made out of frangipani flowers. Kay and I gave Dave a big cockroach corpse we found in the back of the carport for his lower form science classes. He loved it.

We have lots of cockroaches here, though we don't see them very often. On evenings when I'm done with my prep and grading, and looking for something exciting to do, I go into the kitchen, flip on the light, and see how many cockroaches I can stomp on before they scurry into their hidey-holes. It's a personal best thing. Kay doesn't get as excited as I do. She prefers to read. You have to make do with what's available.

Harriet

FRIDAY, FEBRUARY 25, 1966

Dear Mom and Pop,

Last weekend Kay, Winnie, Steve, and I went to Tabora, a small town south of here, for the wedding of our PCV friends, Diane and Bernie. We were worried about roads being rained out, but when we left, the weather seemed fine. We nominated Steve to drive because he drove a VW bug like Kay's from Peru to the U.S. on his way home from his first Peace Corps experience.

Tabora is 278 km from Mwanza, which is about 172 miles. We planned to spend a night in Shinyanja, about halfway to Tabora, but we had not contacted anyone there before we left Mwanza, around 4:30 p.m. The Williamson Diamond Mine is sixteen miles this side of Shinyanja, and John Wenge of my group was assigned to teach at the new secondary school, but the buildings had not been finished when we left Dar. We weren't sure where the school was located, if it was open, or even if John had arrived.

When we got there, we poked around the mine fences, which were serious fences. Security at the diamond mines is tight. When the lights inside around the equipment and mine buildings started to go out, we decided the school must not be inside the fence, so we went on to Shinyanja.

We were almost there when we passed an upper primary school right on the road. I got out our *Guide to Peace Corps Volunteers,* which listed two PCVs who were teaching there, so we knocked on their door. We were hoping for an invitation to stay the night, but they gave us coffee and directions to our next stop without the offer. We moved on, a little worried because it was getting quite late.

On the train to Mwanza, I'd met a religious sister who was starting the commercial school in the next town. She'd told me to come and see her if I got to the area, so I did, with my three friends, at 10:30 p.m. We were getting desperate.

The sisters were just going to bed, but they were gracious and seemed glad to have company. We begged for floor space and they were happy to accommodate us. After more coffee, we sacked out on the concrete porch. It was a bit firm, but we were so tired we slept fine. They prepared an excellent breakfast and showed us around their not-yet-opened school. They were very proud of it, so we oohed and aahed. They were really in a remote part of town, and if I had been them, any visitors would have been welcomed. The next morning, we thanked the nuns profusely before we left.

With no directions for finding our friends in Tabora, we searched for schools, which all have a playing field and are not difficult to find in a small town. When we found the school, we stopped at the first house to ask directions to the wedding. To our surprise, we found the groom (Bernie) making his final preparations inside! He was startled and glad to see us because we were the only people who had come from out of town.

We changed clothes quickly and had ten minutes to spare before the wedding started in a large church. The reception that night was low-key, which was fine with me. The next morning, we visited the happy couple in their new home and then started back to Mwanza.

It had rained while we were in Tabora, and the roads were muddy but not too squishy yet. Steve did well driving on the rough, washboard-like roads. The rest of us were able to grab a little sleep. After a nap, I was enjoying the scenery and a breeze from the open window when we passed a big truck. It hit a huge puddle, and I got a face full of muddy water.

We were home by dark. Kay and I discovered her cat with her new kittens...on *my* pillow! *Yech!* I had to clean up the mess. The cat loves my pillow and I had been willing to share, but really, that was just too much. So, now we know that the cat is a female and she *was* pregnant. It wasn't worms, which would have been *really* disgusting on my pillow! But that wouldn't have happened. She is a bit more discreet than that. Each of the three kittens is a different color, and must have had a different father. We now have one black and white kitten, a tabby, and a grey one. That hussy.

This week's excitement has been the lake flies, a bit like mosquitoes but much more delicate and no biting. They hatch when it rains, and on Wednesday night it rained very hard. On our way to class in the morning we saw a huge brown cloud on the horizon, roiling like an approaching storm. At the break we were sipping our cups of hot, milky tea and nibbling our sweet biscuits when I looked out the window and noticed it was getting dark. I thought it was just heavy rain, but there was no sound. Shirley saw me looking, and gasped, "Lake flies!" Everyone ran to the windows.

The cloud of insects blotted out the other side of the courtyard, maybe fifty feet away. We scrambled to close all the windows, but it was too late. The tiny insects filled our classrooms. They got in my nose and mouth, and made it hard to breathe.

At night, the flies gathered in busy clouds around lights only to die and fall into deep, fluffy heaps on the floor and sills of our porch windows. The students say that some local people make the flies into patties and fry them, and they taste like fish. Most of the girls don't live on the lake and think that eating them is an awful idea. I do, too.

When it was raining so hard, I wore my poncho as usual, and most of the girls had nothing to keep them dry to get to the physics-with-chemistry lab for class. They usually put their textbooks over their heads and run fast, but the rain was pelting so hard I lent them my poncho. They ferried themselves to my lab in little rafts of six, clutching each other in a giggling clump. They think my poncho and high boots look quite funny, but they are willing to use them. I don't mind. A little diversion is welcome.

Last night I saw *My Fair Lady* at our local theater. This is a roaring town! We let some students cut grass around our house so they could earn the two shillings to go to the movie. About one hundred upper-form girls went to see *My Fair Lady* because they studied *Pygmalion* in Kay's class. They really enjoyed it. After being in Tabora and Shinyanga, this feels like the center of a cultural universe.

I have no fear now of hyenas and leopards. Often, I see them, and they just run away. Either I am too big, or they aren't hungry enough. I saw monkeys and rock hyraxes in a tree when I was walking the other evening. The hyraxes climb the rock mounds and step right onto the tree branches. They look like little furry pigs walking high off the ground. Very strange. I'd like to see one up close, but they are very flighty.

I looked up hyraxes in my mammal book and the closest biological relative to a hyrax is an elephant(!) due to the fact that their testicles descend into the scrotum only when they are breeding. Pretty remote relationship, if you ask me. When I told Steve this amazing fact, he got a funny, pained expression on his face.

Harriet

TUESDAY, MARCH 8, 1966

Dear Everyone,

You asked about the leopard (or at least you should have). Well, the game wardens set a trap last week near the playing field. I went down to check it out. The trap was a long, thin, metal cage of thick mesh, baited inside, like a giant squirrel trap. When the animal enters, the trap springs shut. The bait was a live chicken tied by its leg. It was in a separate compartment so the leopard couldn't get it, but I wonder if anyone mentioned that to the chicken.

Thursday on my way up to the classrooms, I was surprised to find a stream of girls flowing down the car track, chattering and gay. Very unusual since they should have been in class. I stopped one and asked what was going on.

"Oh, Miss Dainsone," that's how they say my name, "Mrs. Makonde gave us permission to leave class because the *askaris* (game wardens) caught the leopard. Come along. She is in the trap."

The student hurried to catch up with her friends, and I followed. A mob of girls surrounded the cage, chattering and jumping with excitement, but in a peculiar way. Somehow, it felt like a victory dance. Over what, I don't know. This poor leopard never hurt anyone, since no one has been injured lately. It just scared the girls when they saw it at night, as she did me. The way the girls acted, you'd have thought she had killed someone, and was a real menace.

I inched my way into the crowd, and they drew back so I could see. I was as thrilled as they were to be so close to a live leopard. The fur looked so soft and the spotted pattern was stunning up close—deep black spots on a rich background of butterscotch to wheat to cream. Much as I would have loved to stroke her, well, I didn't. The game wardens said she had cubs somewhere because she was full of milk. I wonder where they are because they will be hungry by now, poor things.

The girls returned to class, but not for long. At about 10:30 a.m., the game department truck came to take the leopard to the Serengeti. This time the entire school, teachers, students, cooks and *shamba* boys (yardworkers) and office staff, trooped down to the field to see her off. The day was heating up, and the leopard's tongue draped down the side of her mouth. Her side almost vibrated, she was panting so hard. She had to be very thirsty. In spite of the curious crowd, she was calm and not fighting the cage. Maybe it was just exhaustion. She had a little blood on her nose, so at some time she must have scraped it, but she had no other injuries. The game wardens had a crane on the back of their truck and lifted her in the trap to the truck bed and off she went to the park. I hope she got to her new home safely.

A few days after, one of the *shamba* boys glimpsed another leopard and a cub during the day. We think it was the father. The *askaris* reset the trap. I hope they catch the cub in the trap with Dad so it doesn't starve. Then I hope they let them go near Mom.

I took Kay's guitar to the school hall last Saturday. Some girls heard me playing the guitar and came in. Six of them had learned some songs with a previous teacher, so they sang them to me. I joined in, and we had a great time. One of the songs stumped me. The words were a total mystery, hardly English, and the tune was a bit mushy. When I heard "diddy, diddy," I finally figured out it was the song "Roses are Red, Dilly

Dilly." "L's" are hard for them to pronounce. I found the song in my songbook and we sang the whole thing together. They were delighted. Then, I sang them the even sillier alphabet song:

"B A Bay" (B E Bee, B I Bickie Bye B O Bo Bickie Bye, etc.).

You go through the alphabet and use new consonants for each verse. They really cracked up at that one and wanted to learn it.

Sometimes, when I put the lights out, I go into the dorms and chat for a while with the students and recently, I've been giving lessons to teach that song. Everyone wants to learn it. During school time, when they pass me I hear mumbles of "B I Bickie By, B O Bo..." and they all laugh.

Sunday morning, I polished some of the songs to sing at a hootenanny that evening, which some volunteers in the area pulled together. I'm one of the three guitar players, and one guy plays a ukulele. I hold my own in the group, and it's great fun. There's quite a group here who sing the same sort of folk songs I learned in my college dorm: Kingston Trio, Peter, Paul and Mary, etc., and we are all learning new songs and chords from each other.

The science club visited one of the two Tanzanian agricultural research centers nearby. It was quite a warm day, and we walked to the top of a rock dome for the class. A blackboard was already set up under a shady tree that grew out of a crack in the rock. Next to it was a table full of soil samples from the region. From the top, we could see the whole valley. Fat clouds passed over, and the light played on the fields below. It was gorgeous.

The instructor lectured on soil, fertilizers, etc. and the main crop here, cotton. I learned you can tell good and bad farming in the local plots by noticing what color of green the crop is. Something's lacking in yellowish green plots. Healthy crops are a deeper green.

I sent some local fabric (it comes in sets of 8 yards) to Mom or Carol to make a blouse or dress. For this area, the pattern is quite conservative, but if you will wear it I will send some of the really snazzy African cloth, which is even more colorful. I also sent Allen a shirt made of the same material. Please tell him it's one of the two styles available. You buy the cloth and have the seamstress in the shop sew it up.

I picked up the international and Oregon driver's licenses you sent, and thank you. Wow. Now I'm mobile. Kay drives and I have the license. It works. Teaching is fine. The Form IV students keep stumping me with questions about electricity. I just thought they were eager, but finally figured out that they were using me rather than looking up their own answers to the questions they have been given by Mrs. Birnie, their physics-with-chemistry teacher. I haven't studied electricity for years, so I had no answers for them on that subject. I do wish my books would get here from Syracuse.

Our Peace Corps conference, April 17-18, falls right in the middle of our two-and-a-half week vacation. The conference is in Dodoma, west of Dar and next to nowhere. I think I'll stay here to bone up on the Form IV material. After this term, when Mrs. Birnie leaves, I will be the senior science staffer, teaching all the upper form sciences. I can also straighten up the lab and there is a lot to do. The physics-with-chemistry lab has built-in cupboards full of things for demonstrations. I can figure out if they still work while I'm cleaning out the old wasp nests and termite tunnels.

The kittens are almost playing now, although their mother gets anxious when we put them on the rug. She wants them in their cozy box. I'm getting used to the wild animals wandering around. I've chased several hyenas down the path away from the garbage. All of them seem afraid of people unless they are cornered or trapped, like the leopard was. Monkeys wander through sometimes. One sat on our driveway and looked in through the front door to check us out. Apparently, we were not interesting enough for a closer inspection.

Harriet

MONDAY, MARCH 14, 1966

Dear Everyone,

Thank you, Mom, for preparing my taxes. Here is what I know: PC teachers in my group get 850 shillings a month as living allowance from the Tanzanian government, about $121.50, but since it's from the Tanzanian government, no U.S. taxes. Not much money, but enough for personal needs. We only pay U.S. taxes on our $75 per month accumulating from the Peace Corps, which we'll receive when we return home. I'm not sure about the $7.50 per day vacation allowance, but since I haven't received any, I won't worry about how to deal with it.

You worry about me being dirty. Kay says Americans have such a "sterile" look about them because they prefer short hair, shaved legs, etc. Actually, cleanliness is no problem. I've finally gotten used to taking baths since we don't have a shower. We have a tank on the wall above the bath and when you turn on the hot water tap, a propane flame ignites and heats just what you need. Pretty neat. We have two, five-gallon propane tanks for the frig, stove, and hot water. When one runs out, we just unhook it and take it into town and fill it.

Juma is surly and he's still a bad cook. He is sick now and can't cook anyway, so we do it. He coughs a lot. It came on suddenly, so I don't think it's tuberculosis, but there is TB in this area. He went to the hospital yesterday and again today. We don't know what he learned, but are being cautious.

Kay has arranged for us to get a new cook. His name is Suleimani, a common Muslim name. He works for Mrs. Berry now, and will be available when she leaves in May. I haven't met him, but Kay is excited, and I'm sure she will be happier with someone who knows how to cater to a Brit. I've never had a cook before now, except my mother! Meanwhile, we have to put up with Juma.

I'm thinking about vacation possibilities with our first school break approaching in April, just two-and-a-half weeks from now. We get another short vacation in August as well. In December, we get about six weeks' vacation, which is the best time to climb Kilimanjaro, but I might wait to do that later. It will be very hot in Dar, but maybe I'll go there for a week this break and visit Zanzibar.

You wouldn't know of any high school students who would like African pen pals, would you? The girls really thirst for firsthand news from anywhere. I don't think any of them have traveled beyond home and school. Geography is a lovely class, but a real live letter from someone in another part of the world is something to be worshiped in its entirety. Tell Allen that if he gets any strange letters from Africa, it's my fault. I broke down and gave his address to some girls who are dying for pen pals, pronounced "pin-palls." They want to correspond with anyone, but especially boys.

Tell Allen if he answers, not to say anything even vaguely suggestive. These girls are so bowled over by letters from anyone they will read all sorts of things into it, especially letters about America. Tell him not to make jokes. They won't understand, and they could easily misinterpret them. I wouldn't be surprised if they asked Allen to pay their way to America just to see him. They figure that any money not their own must be easy to come by. Their families pay school fees, so they don't handle much money. Any price more than the price of a bar of soap is the same to them.

All is well.

Harriet

SUNDAY, MARCH 27, 1966

Dear Family,

Carol, the TV show you mentioned, *Daktari*, must take place somewhere near Mt. Kilimanjaro. Speaking of which, I just wrote to see if I could assist the girls' session of the Outward Bound Mountain School located on the Kilimanjaro slopes. The school involves four to six weeks of training, climbing, hiking, etc., and the climax is the five-day climb up the mountain from the northeast. Since it's for girls, I think I can do it. I hope I can.

You asked about my schedule. Every day is different. This term is about over, but here's an idea. Classes last 40 minutes each, starting at 8 a.m. The teachers move between classrooms unless it's a class with equipment, e.g. science class, cooking, sewing or typing, then the students have to come to the special rooms. There's a pot of tea with milk and biscuits from 10 to 10:30, then classes until 12:30, followed by lunch until 2, then three more classes in the afternoon until 4p.m.

Of course, we have tea after classes end, a very British custom. I'm getting used to the milky tea and the cookies—biscuits, really, not sweet like a cookie.

Kay calls them "bickies." It's kind of nice, the afternoon tea gives us a chance to chat and unwind from
the day. Some of the teachers don't come, which is
too bad, and we don't see much of them, mostly the
Africans. Makes sense, since tea isn't their thing,
but we are a small community and it's hard to get to
know someone who seems to avoid the staff room. The
African teachers' houses are in a different part of the
compound, so it's hard to just "drop by." Then there is
the language problem. My Swahili and their English
are at the same rudimentary level.

This term I'm only teaching 20 periods out of 45
possible in a week, a lighter load than most regular
teachers because I'm new. I get to learn the science
ropes from Mrs. Birnie. Some teachers come with no
overlap, so I'm lucky. After school on Mondays, Mrs.
Birnie oversees the science club, which I'll inherit.

Thursdays, I take athletics with the girls. It's track
and field, running, jumping, throwing. Kind of fun.
Their last coach left a while ago, and they haven't had
anyone since, so I volunteered. Better me than no one
at all. Plus, I have always wanted to figure out how to
throw a discus. It doesn't look very hard. Running is running, so that shouldn't be too difficult. Some of the older
girls are pretty good at the events and can help me out.
One student, Esther, even went to the Commonwealth
Games in Jamaica a couple of years ago. Attendance is
voluntary, but there is still a good turnout. Otherwise,
there is nothing physical for the girls to do.

Every other Wednesday I'm on duty for study
period from 7 to 8:30 at night, and then I do lights
out at 9:30. I'm also on duty three days per term, one
Friday, and a Saturday and Sunday. When I am on
duty, I just have to stay at the school for problems
that might arise, and to chase away the boys who
wander down from the boys' school. It isn't a hard

task for me since I live here, but it's less convenient for Mrs. Birnie, who lives in town with her husband. She brings books to read and hangs out in the staff room grading papers, or she visits us.

It's not as humid as it was when I arrived, and I have more energy. The temperature now is perfect, cool if anything, and an occasional sweater feels good. It doesn't take much of a drop in temperature for everyone to start complaining of a cold snap. Even when it's raining, it's nice. We have had more rain lately, but the clouds come and go, and the sun returns.

The vacation schedule is terribly confusing now. Someone higher up made a change, and now, Monday is a public holiday. It's rumored the girls will go home early. How early? Who knows? I had planned to give tests, but we must collect books.

When school does close, I'm going to a two-week science course for teachers in Dar at the University College. I toured it when we first arrived. It's out of town a ways, built on a hill to catch a lovely breeze.

Can you send me the *Life Magazine* nature series? It really has terrific pictures, and any zoology text would help. The British high school texts here don't cover everything. In addition, they are written for the English climate (and culture, I might add). A lesson that strikes me as especially inappropriate for these students is the one on condensation: "When steam rises from your bath, note how it condenses on the cold water spout." These girls only have access to showers, just lukewarm out of the tap, which feels good when it's hot outside. No steam condenses on anything metal because it doesn't get cold enough. Ever. I'll have to boil some water and find a glass to demonstrate this strange idea.

Lately, I've been climbing. Quite fun. It takes about ten minutes, leaping boulder to boulder, to reach the top of a rock mound right next to my house.

Sometimes, the boulders are too far apart, and I touch the ground between, kind of like cheating. I can see the whole school from the top, and when I turn my back, there's nothing but water. No one else likes to do this kind of stuff so I'm all alone and love it, just me and the lizards. Mrs. Berry told me that years ago another teacher was wandering around on the rocks, and she was killed by a boa constrictor, so I'll keep my eyes open. Did I mention the big lizards? They have eight-inch blue bodies with long tails, sit on hot rocks or on school roofs, and bob their orangey-red heads.

Higher ridges separate us from the valleys on either side, and I climb up them, too. Cattle paths all over, but sometimes they peter out into some delicious grassy area. The other day I watched a couple of men digging a pit, wide and shallow. A few days later they filled it up with wood. There are not many large trees around, and now I know why: they're cut to make charcoal, which the woodcutters then sell. The wood is carefully stacked crisscross in the pit, covered with dirt and set afire to smolder for days in the oxygen-depleted air. Some days, I can see the thin string of smoke from the house.

When I returned to the spot, just a few charcoal bits were scattered in the empty pit. Men walk the road with huge sisal bags full of charcoal balanced on their heads, or on bicycles. Sometimes, several shoulder-high bags are propped together at the side of the road. I don't know if people buy them there, or if they are waiting for a truck to pick them up.

Flame trees and jacarandas grow around the school. When the flame trees (flamboyant) bloom, clusters of small but intensely orange flowers cover them. Now, huge old flat pods dangle open from last year's seeds. You can shake them like a rattle. The jacaranda is similar, but with clusters of medium blue flowers and flat, round pods. After the flowers have impressed everyone, the leaves emerge. The trees cast a deep shade, which is what I enjoy now.

I tried your recipe for brown sugar brownies but would you check the amount of flour? The recipe says to use two-thirds of a cup, which makes them like candy, not how I remember them.

I just got your letter. The *kitenge* cloth I sent is made in Holland and Japan, for sale in Africa only. You can't get it anywhere else at these prices. The Dutch cloth is a better quality than the cloth for *kangas* and comes in stunningly colorful patterns. It is especially good for a straight shift dress. One pattern is the Tanzania national cloth, which women wear in a number of ways on national holidays. Like most patterns, it is based on a rectangle with wide and complex borders and a center pattern. The national cloth has kind of a big eye shape in the middle.

There's a better selection of cloth in Dar, so I'll get more when I'm there.

Harriet

Captured leopard.

CHAPTER THREE

First School Break

Dear Family,

School closed a week earlier than we'd planned. Three religious holidays were coming up in a row, so Mrs. King'ori, our new headmistress, decided to send the girls home on Saturday, April 2. The girls on the athletics (track & field) team stayed that day for the meet.

Vehicles were overbooked with girls going to buses, trains, or the boat, and others were going to the track meet. Saturday morning I waited for an available lorry and chewed my nails. We have to check for books in the departing girls' baggage. So, I made myself useful. One of the teachers took pity on me and drove the earliest competitors to the meet in her car.

The lorry finally arrived and the rest of us piled in. There was no top, so when rain burst from the skies, we all got soaked. At the track, the meet had paused for the rain, but even with some shelter, everyone was wet because it had arrived so quickly. I was told to go to the outfield to mark shot put throws. You can dodge a shot, but the big splash when it hits the ground can still get you. By the time the competition ended, I was dripping in mud. At dusk, I was marking javelin throws, a death-defying job. Javelins zoomed at me out of the dark. The field had no lights, but the meet continued until it was pitch black. We just had to make do—and duck.

We have a natural runner at our school. Esther was legman for the relay. When she got the baton, we were in last place. She took off like a gazelle and with each stride, passed one more person. The team finished in second place! Quite amazing. And I'm supposed to train her? Ha!

Sunday, the last of the girls left for home. The same day, Roger Howard, one of the boys in my PCV group from Mbeya, arrived escorting some students on the train. He had to stay until Tuesday for the return trip, so he stayed at Steve Sterk's house down the road.

On Monday, six of us took off on a hike with no particular destination in mind. Inside a jumble of massive rocks we shimmied up through the open spaces. Quite fun. I got lots of scratches, but didn't see any boas.

Now, I'm in Dar, attending the science course I mentioned a while ago. I arrived by train on Monday, delayed six hours due to a five-car derailment (not our train!). The college bus met me, but I was the only one to arrive and the dorms weren't ready. I left my stuff at the college and went into town for a few hours to wait. The course runs this Tuesday to next Tuesday, an odd arrangement, but maybe it fits some schools' vacation schedules. I don't ask.

I saw Peace Corps Volunteers everywhere; we have a "look." It was fun to visit with others from my group and everyone's glad the first term is over. Now, we are experienced teachers.

Today at a break in the course, I discovered that nine of us weren't even expected by the college. They found beds for us anyway—so we are 48 total. Except for three PCVs, the students are career teachers: Indians, Africans, and Catholic nuns and brothers.

The course will be like the physics Allen took in high school. You have to discover what concept we are studying instead of just being told the facts. Learning how to teach it should be fun. I feel a step ahead of the others, since I was not raised in the British rote learning system, which is probably why no one asks questions.

I may go to Zanzibar on Sunday.

Harriet

SUNDAY, APRIL 24, 1966

Dear Family,

The science course here is okay although it drags during the hot afternoons. Friday, we were to study the proboscis action of a fly, basically, when he sticks out his tongue. My fly did it a few times. I understood what he was doing, and studying it all afternoon seemed "a bit much" (Kay's phrase).

Anne Wiggins and I decided to leave the course a little early Friday to go to the Peace Corps conference in Dodoma, about 400 km (220 miles) east of here. Ten of our Tanzania X group rode together on the bus and used the nine-hour trip to catch up.

The first night was pretty crowded since some PCVs from another conference hadn't left yet. There were 48 beds and 50 people, but someone had brought a camp bed and one person was on the floor.

Not too much was accomplished during the formal meetings, but I really enjoyed talking to the others.

We haven't seen each other since we arrived, so it was fun to find out what they were doing. We all have some issues, like poor teachers, discipline problems, and shortage of supplies. A few are in really remote places and have to travel a day just to get their shopping done. I'm pretty lucky to be so near a major town. We can find most of what we need in Mwanza.

I saw Kay, my housemate, a few times in Dodoma. She had gone to Mpwapwa to see her boyfriend. After her visit, she was headed for Dar and rolled her Volkswagen over, so she came back to Dodoma for repairs. No injuries, luckily. She should be back in Mwanza by now. By the way, Winnie told me two letters of yours await me in Mwanza. She didn't bring them because I wasn't certain I would show up here when I left Mwanza.

When the conference ended, Anne W. and I needed to get back to Dar to finish our course, so we got a ride in a Peace Corps vehicle. We saw about 20 giraffes on the road. I don't know if we were near a game park, but then, the animals don't know where they are either.

If we hadn't gotten that ride, we would have taken the bus with others. We learned at the PC office that the bus had smashed head-on into a lorry. Four first-class passengers were killed. Pretty gruesome. We PCVs always go second class, the back of the bus, which was a good thing. All my friends were fine except Lou Bufano, who broke his nose in the accident. Bad luck for Lou because he broke his foot in training.

On the trip from Dodoma I had an attack of malaria. I didn't get much sympathy because everyone else has had it several times already. They said the change of climate from Mwanza to Dar is supposed to bring on malaria if you have it in your blood. You get what feels like a cold and are weak, making it likely the malaria will flare up. I was pretty miserable for a couple of days, with a wretched headache and chills, but the Aralia (chloroquine) knocked it out quickly, so I'm fine. I've been bitten by so many mosquitoes I'm surprised I haven't gotten it before this. Anne and Scott Wallace, who teach here in town, both live in high malarial zones. Mwanza is not one.

Since my train to go back to Mwanza doesn't leave Dar until Thursday at 2 p.m., Anne, Scott, and I are going to Zanzibar. We leave early Wednesday.

Fritz Snyder wanted to come with us, but he was bitten by a dog before going to Dodoma and he has to stay in Dar to get his rabies shots. They're injected in the stomach, and he says they really hurt. I'll avoid dogs. He said it was a mom with pups. It probably wasn't rabid, but the Peace Corps is very protective, so he has to take the whole series of rabies shots.

The weather here on the coast is too hot, but occasionally becomes bearable. Here at the university, the breeze is lovely, but in town, I know, it is quite muggy.

Harriet

SATURDAY, APRIL 30, 1966

Dear Family,

Today, I arrived back in Mwanza after a 44 1/2 hour train trip, only six hours late. Suleimani, our new cook, is now on the job. I'll let you know how he works out.

Lots to tell first!

The seminar ended Tuesday at 4 p.m. Anne and I went into town and stayed at the Peace Corps hostel. We had dinner at Margo's, a nice restaurant with safe steaks that I can order medium rare. Well done is dry and unappetizing. I don't like steaks that way even if they are safer.

Wednesday morning we got up at six to meet Scott at the airport. After a short flight across the Zanzibar Channel to the town of Zanzibar on the island of Zanzibar (whew), a man from the travel agency helped us through customs and took us to the hotel for breakfast. We three were taken to the travel agency with an old lady. It seems she was to go with us on our tour, but she was quite grumpy, so we complained and got rid of her. On our tour around the town the guide drove us past several old estates and the government farm where they grow samples of everything cultivated on the island; cinnamon, cloves, coffee, tea, and ylang-ylang. Flowers of the ylang-ylang are used in perfumes.

We visited a place where they prepare copra, the coconut flesh for export. At the clove distillery, the aroma knocked me back it was so strong. Yum! It was an interesting tour with everything explained in Swahili. Scott's Swahili is the best, so he helped Anne and me when we didn't catch what was said. I don't think the other lady would have enjoyed it at all. Her taxi passed us, in fact, so she was probably seeing most of the same things. Maybe they gave her an English-speaking guide.

After lunch, we walked around the town and got delightfully lost. Most of the narrow streets are too skinny for cars, but bicycles rip through at a high speed. On the wider streets, you have to jump into a doorway to let the horn-blaring cars pass. The streets are the exact width of one car plus three inches.

We found an Ismaeli mosque, built for a branch of Shia Islam. Some old men showed us their upper room, a huge chamber, very clean, with mats on the floor. A large square bed filled one corner, covered with plush silk pillows. Above it hung a photo of the Aga Khan in anticipation of a visit. He is the head of the largest

Shiite sect. I don't think he ever has visited, but they are ready. He finances the Aga Khan Boys' School in Mwanza as he does many others in towns where the sect is strong. Downstairs, a bunch of women sang in a bored, whining, nasal monotone. I wondered if they were reciting the Koran.

We wandered some more. Hoping for a city view from the belfry of a church, we tried the door, but the staff wouldn't let us up the stairs. After dinner, we bought some souvenirs. I got two carved boxes, an Alexandrite stone, and an ivory fan all for around $25. Thursday morning, we looked up one of our Swahili teachers from our Syracuse training who is teaching in a secondary school in Zanzibar City. She just married the Minister of Finance for Zanzibar, the island, which was a country but recently joined Tanganyika to become Tanzania. We had quite an enjoyable time, and were glad we spent the night for the extra time to nose around rather than making just a day trip.

We flew back to Dar in time to catch my train.

Lots of letters were waiting for me when I returned to Mwanza, so here are some answers to questions from your last four letters: Only Shirley has a radio, but it doesn't get much world news; most of our news comes through *Newsweek,* the one with flimsy pages. Shirley passes on her *New York Times* Sunday supplement.

The meat we can buy is mediocre. There are two cuts of beef. We buy filets (all the letters in the word pronounced) at thirty-five cents a pound, which can be made edible, though sometimes it's pretty tough. *Moja moja* is everything else cut into chunks, so named because it's one shilling for one kilo, or six cents a pound. This meat is very tough. There are no other cuts. Kay buys the stewing meat for dog meat, which she feeds Freya. I think it is a bit rude when she orders "dog meat" rather than *moja moja,* since most people eat it themselves.

The fish we can buy is tilapia, three to four fish for one dollar. If the gills are bright red, it's fresh. One fish is a meal for one person. The chicken is passable for variety if cooked in a stew, though seeing it hanging with tons of flies on it is rather off-putting. (That's one of Kay's expressions.) Better to buy a live one and have the cook kill it. They look so scrawny, even with all their feathers on. We don't do that very often.

As a note, a week's worth of fruit and vegetables costs about a dollar, and we eat lots in season. We buy bananas—the small, very sweet ones—and juicy oranges. Mangos are cheap because there are mango trees everywhere. I love mangos and could eat two or three a day. Travelers prepare them by slicing through the fruit as close to the flat seed as possible. They score the bright orange meat and push from the skin side, turning it all inside out. The cubes stick up on the inverted skin, perfect for bites. The mango trees are huge with thick, rounded tops and lovely shade beneath. Papayas grow on the school grounds, but I think someone owns them. One skinny papaya tree grows at our backdoor and has a single papaya on it. We buy most of them at the market. They are bigger than footballs! The long orange slices are sooo delicious with a squirt from the tiny local limes.

The girls live in four spartan dormitories with metal bunk beds. I suspect girls from the same region sleep together in the dorms because they are not segregated by what form they are in. The girls do their best to make their personal area homey. Each one has a suitcase or a trunk for her stuff. There is a shower/toilet building between each pair of dorms, with washing troughs on the outside wall for washing faces and clothing.

Everyone calls them girls, but it feels strange. A few of the girls in the upper forms are not that much younger than I am. The older ones are quite mature and very serious students. Space for qualified girls in secondary school is limited. Few who finish primary school are able to attend secondary school. A handful of the girls don't seem to take their studies seriously and I wonder how they got in. Connections carry a lot of weight. I have my suspicions. The girls can leave the property only with a teacher or with special permission. A popular pastime for them is to braid each other's hair. Some of the designs are stunning: rows, coils, and a variety of designs that boggle the mind. The braids will stay tight for several weeks before becoming a bit ratty-looking and need to be redone.

Carol, I am glad you are planning to visit. I sent brochures for the trips to Treetops and the Serengeti, and holidays in East Africa. I don't go on safaris, so to share my experience, you may have to give up tours and physical comfort and just let come what may. The things you see, the people you'll meet, and what you learn will more than make up for any slight discomfort.

Regarding the PCV who was killed: her husband is being held here in Mwanza on a murder charge by the Tanzanian government. Those who know him can't imagine him killing his wife. They'd been married about a year. Tanzania only has one kind of murder charge, no first-degree or second-degree, etc. We have had no news for several weeks about this.

I don't know about the Kilimanjaro program yet. Not a peep from Outward Bound, but I'll let you know as soon as I do.

School starts Tuesday.

Harriet

Students on a field trip, waiting for the boat to Saa Nane Island, a small wildlife sanctuary on the SE shore of Lake Victoria.

CHAPTER FOUR

Second School Term

SATURDAY, MAY 7, 1966

Dear Allen and All,

I have launched my career as a senior science mistress. Four classes with 140 students total have now been exposed to "discovery science" from my class in Dar. One class is learning photosynthesis and the other, transpiration, closely related subjects. Each student has to do an experiment. It really bugs them because they haven't a clue what to do. I asked, "Do plants transpire at night?" They don't know, so I say, "Well, why don't you use that as your experiment?"

At first, they groan, but once the experiment crystallizes, they are quite pleased to tell me the answer. The majority of the students seem interested. I don't think they have ever done experiments with unknown outcomes. I have to spend a lot of time in preparation so they will be able to do the work, but it is still interesting.

The kittens are about eleven weeks old and quite lively. My favorite is a fluffy black male with tiny white paws. Kay named him Pierre, but I call him Bear Face or Fluff the Tough. Every time you approach him he puts up his dukes.

Kay fired Juma when I was in Dar and Suleimani is our new cook. He is wonderful, quite cheerful, and much more pleasant to have around than Juma, who did not improve his cooking even with Kay's coaching. When Kay fired him, Juma refused to vacate the room in the carport where he often slept. Suleimani had to leave our house at 5 p.m. and walk home. Kay and I did our own dinner. Juma finally moved out and Suleimani found Kay's missing tablecloth and several napkins in that room.

Winnie, Kay, and I went to town Tuesday. I discovered that a 100 shillings note was missing from my wallet, so I had to go to the bank for some cash. I think it was Juma.

Suleimani is a good cook, trained in the English way anyway, one of Kay's primary criteria. Stocky and a little shorter than I am, he always wears his white Muslim men's dress and usually a cap when he's working. Hard to tell how old Suleimani is, but he has lots of grandchildren to his obvious pleasure. He takes his whites off to walk home when he doesn't spend the night here. I don't know how far it is, but the walk doesn't faze him. He calls both of us Mama, uncomfortable for me because he could be my grandfather. In Swahili, it means I could be a mama—not that I am one, which is also unnerving.

Harriet

SATURDAY, MAY 14, 1966

Dear Mom and Pop,
Juma is trying to get some money from us because of the way we let him go. Kay fired him but it was while I

was away so I don't know the details. We certainly let him know his work wasn't great.

On Friday, Kay and I went to court and found out that the case was called Thursday and reset since no one was there. Of course, we weren't there: no one had notified the labor officer or us. Anyway, we talked to the officer and he understood our side. We were supposed to give a one-month notice or one month's pay, which we refused to do. We would have settled except that Juma, who turned up by chance, would not agree to anything. We finally saw his problem. His wife just lost her job because her employer left. Juma didn't want to have to look for another job. We settled for one month's work as a *shamba* boy with pay, and he finally agreed. He'll be sorry. Our yard is a mess. If he is lazy, we can cut him off with no notice.

Shamba boys ("boy" has nothing to do with age, a holdover from colonial use) are yardmen. Some are skilled and can create a nice garden, but most just cut the lawn. "Cut" and "lawn" are stretching the terms. Ours is a mass of wild grass between our house and the lake. It can be so lush we sometimes find cattle enjoying a munch. There is nothing intentional about it, but if it dries up, it is a fire hazard.

Yardmen cut the lawns by hand. The tool they use is a springy piece of thin metal, about two inches wide and four feet long. It looks like it could be a spring of some sort. They bend the end into a slow curve and sharpen both sides of the tip. The worker stands and swings it side-to-side, grass flying high in the air as the blade carries it to the end of the stroke. One man can whip through a field of grass in no time.

Did you read about the slaving going on in Kenya and Tanzania? Gad, it's hard to believe.

I found the missing 100 shillings in my camera lens case so Juma didn't steal it as I had suspected. I stick my extra cash in my socks, shoe bags, and other safe places, but I need to remember where I put things. Thank you for the birth certificate. Kay might get her driving license soon.

Harriet

SATURDAY, MAY 21, 1966

Dear Mom,

Yesterday, I took a group of biology students to Saa Nane, a tiny island in Smith's Sound, fifteen minutes by slow boat from Mwanza. It is an open game park with pens for the less reliable animals: ostriches, rhinos, buffaloes, hunting dogs, porcupines, otters, and birds that would fly away unless their wings were clipped. Dikdiks (small deer the size of a spaniel), deer, zebras, giraffes, and many other animals wander at will, uninterested in visitors. There are no great herds. The island is tiny and every animal has to be brought by boat, but it is the beginning of a nice little zoo. It seems odd that many Africans have not seen wild animals beyond the local hyenas, rock rabbits (hyraxes), and the occasional leopard. Even in the Serengeti, you can't get too close, but few of the locals get out there either.

Only the dikdik was aggressive. The gamekeeper said he doesn't like large crowds. Yesterday, we were there with a group from one of the Indian schools. A crowd I'd say with kids spread out all over the island. When the dikdik first arrived on the island, he started butting people when he got annoyed. Since he had little sharp horns, he must have injured someone because the gamekeepers cut them off. However, he still attacks visitors, as much as that tiny thing can. His back is knee-high to an adult, so when he lowers his head, watch out. He lurks in the grass and when people turn away from him, he races out to butt them.

I was standing next to one of my students and chatting when I looked away for a moment. I turned back and she was gone. I looked down and she was lying on the ground, laughing. No one, it seems, can remain upright after a butt in the back of the knees by the dikdik. It really was quite funny. I kept my eye on him to avoid being a target, but he really was sneaky. He waited until no one was watching and, clippity, clippity, pow! Someone else bit the dust.

Fruit is cheap now. Citrus fruits are five cents each, which is less than one U.S. cent. Good eggplant and tomatoes are 21 cents per pound.

Do you still have our copy of the *World Book Encyclopedia?* Diana Graham, a TEA, has been trying to get a copy for the school with no success. She would be ecstatic if you would send them and bill her for shipping, which Teachers for East Africa will pay for. Peace Corps sent a beautiful set of absolutely worthless technical reference books that no one can understand, even me. Someone else sent the *Encyclopedia Britannica,* which is equally difficult for the girls. We have a *Golden Book Encyclopedia,* which is fine for Form I students. *The World Book* would be perfect.

Harriet

TUESDAY, MAY 31, 1966

Dear All,

Coaching athletics (track and field events) is really fun. The girls don't have many activities outside of school-related stuff and they don't get any exercise at all. I will try to build up this team, which means more than one day of practice a week. Membership will be competitive. All team members can be challenged by others for their position.

What appeals to the girls is getting nice uniforms and shoes. I think I can get Peace Corps to pay half if the girls raise the other half. Any suggestions how? It must be their effort. This is my extracurricular project for now.

I'm getting into the swing of teaching again. It's less of a burden for me to prepare lessons. First term, I was just one step ahead of the students. Thanks to Mr. Foulk's biology class in high school, it wasn't difficult to learn what I was supposed to teach, but still I had to learn that. I have the advantage over the girls for whom English is at least their second language if not third. They may speak a tribal language until primary school. Then they learn Swahili. Primary schools often have students who speak several languages. They will all need Swahili eventually. They begin English after three or four years when they get to upper primary. When I taught Form I Biology, it was really an English class using biology as the topic of conversation. We all understand that, but the material is repeated later, so they don't miss out.

More problems with the ex-cook, Juma. Kay and I had to go back to court. The officer who helped us with the new contract wasn't there and neither was the contract. Everyone concerned seems to have forgotten about it. To top it off, Juma claims he never returned as a *shamba* boy to work out the month's notice, which means he thinks we still owe him. That is a fat lie, but the case was adjourned until the officer we want returns. The judge, a Nigerian, was obviously quite bored with the whole thing. So was I. Juma can't win, but it takes up our time and patience. *Really!* He was so slow to learn and sulky to boot.

I may be able to get rubber cement here under another name. Hold off on sending any for now. Witch doctors? No, just me. I used a press-on patch to repair a hole in a blouse. Suleimani watched with interest, but I could tell he was wondering what in hell I was doing. When he washed the blouse he had to show me how marvelous the patch was because it didn't fall off. I wonder who repairs his clothes. He has several wives. Most Africans have a set of grubby work clothes that have been patched many times over, patches on patches. Sometimes the men will wear two pairs of shorts at once to keep everything covered. I wonder if they are the bachelors.

The Peace Corps doctor called me in because I've been using all his nasal spray. He wants to find out the "real cause" of my sinus problem. More power to him. Anyway, I'm taking Sinutab pills. They help, but not totally because I forget to take them.

Mosquitoes are bad. The rain comes in half-hour torrents every three to four days now, so they hatch out.

Harriet

TUESDAY, JUNE 7, 1966

Dear Family,

Oh how cruel, telling me I haven't written. You probably got my letter right after you sent the one I have in my hand.

I only have 140 pupils this term: four forms at 35 students per form. I just got the *Life* books you sent. They will be a great help. Wonderful pictures. We have midyear exams next week, which means review this week. The Form IVs are reviewing things for the Mock

Cambridge exam, which I didn't teach. I have them write their questions and give them to me. I look up the answers and explain the next day. Today was the first day with that regimen, and I did okay. I need a quick course on Hydra, the ear, and a few other things.

I set up this system of written questions because when I was in training, I was an intern in a high school physics class in Syracuse. One day, the teacher told me I could go over the homework with the class, and he left the room. I think I had been warned, so I went through one of the problems that a student requested. Someone asked another question. I ad-libbed through quite possibly a meaningless explanation with practiced confidence. Inside, I counted the seconds to the end of the class. I only hoped the students knew less than I did, but wasn't certain that was the case. The good/bad news was that some of my fellow PCVs from another school that had a day off were there to watch me teach. Oh, goody. They said I did a convincing job of "BS-ing" my way through. I'd rather not have to do that too often.

Yesterday, I performed my first demonstration dissection on a fish, one I'd bought whole from the market. I had Suleimani just cut off the filet and leave the rest for me to operate on in class. The organs were interesting to point to and pull out for our inspection, but girls kept asking where the lateral line was, a sensory area along the side. I said I ate it, which I didn't exactly do because it's on the skin of the filet. They laughed. Anyway, I saved some of the fish parts for the second class the next afternoon.

This morning the girls complained and said we must move outside because of the rotting fish odor, but I said no, I had to smell the same thing. Suddenly, pow! I was smacked by a cloud of putrid air. The fish left the room.

A few days ago, Kay, Winnie, and I were in an auto

accident on the outskirts of Mwanza. Miss Jevons, another teacher, was driving us to a meeting in her car. A guy on a motorcycle came wobbling in our direction. He was some sort of priest or minister (wearing a dog-collar) and was busy waving at his flock on either side of the road. Coming toward us and not looking where he was going, he swerved right into Miss Jevons' car. She was driving extremely slowly, fortunately. He fell off his bike and wasn't at all injured. There was only minor damage to the vehicles, but the surrounding multitudes (no doubt enjoying the excitement) insisted on calling the police. Miss Jevons agreed, "For insurance purposes."

We all had to appear in court about this several times. The court seemed to enjoy making as much fuss about it as possible. Maybe they needed something to keep them busy. At one point, the West African magistrate (judge) decided that we would all have to travel out to what he called (inaccurately, we didn't hesitate to point out) "the scene of the crime."

So there we all were, standing in the middle of the dirt road: the judge, the minister, Miss Jevons, the three of us, plus various officials from the courthouse. Of course, a crowd gathered, some of them obviously on very friendly terms with the "injured party," the minister. Because she'd been sitting in the front seat, Winnie had the best view of what had happened. She explained what she saw and the minister disagreed. They argued until she gestured to the crowd and houses around and shouted, "You weren't looking where you were going! You were waving to all the people!"

That did it. The judge got the picture right away. He said, "Oh, I see." It more or less ended right then and there.

Miss Jevons is the new typing and shorthand teacher for the Form I classes. Her classroom is up the hill in a space like my labs. The program is new. Our school will eventually graduate many girls with secretarial skills, something needed by this developing country. From what I can see, Miss Jevons is a rather stern English woman who seems angry all the time. Her body is short and stocky like English detective ladies. She only comes to the staff room for mandatory meetings and hangs out in her classroom. We all know when she is approaching because her thick, orthopedic shoes clump, clump, clump on the hard dirt.

I was delighted that Miss Jevons had issued rulers to all the girls, but when I asked them if they could use them in maths (I'm teaching Form I mathematics), they all said she told them only to use them in her class, no one else's. She keeps to herself and seems to have no friends. I feel sorry for her because she really doesn't have any peers, at school, anyway. She is older than most of us and seems permanent to the school system. Most of us are volunteers and contract people who will leave after two years. In our conversations, an opinion has gone around that many of the long-term Brits here are people who could not make it at home and come to Africa to "be somebody." It seems to be true of the missionaries and, I might guess, Miss Jevons.

On Fridays, we have an extra period at the end of the day for *dini* (religion), which is a required subject. Missionaries show up to teach: Catholics, Seventh-Day Adventists, Methodists, and a few others. Someone comes for the Muslim girls as well. Kay volunteered to teach a class in Comparative Religions, and a good number turned out for that, the "unchurched," I guess.

Well, I've begun a great project with the "athleticians." That's what the girls in the athletics program call themselves. Like beauticians? I don't know. I had a meeting with the girls, and they decided to practice two times a week. They will allow a certain number of absences. They have a sergeant at arms to take the role, etc. I hope they really get enthused because I get exercise, too. One girl who comes is very cranky. I appointed her the roll taker, so maybe she'll cheer up. It seems to be working so far. At least she's too busy to complain, which was all she was doing. She's a curiosity to me, because she doesn't have to come at all.

I attended a meeting for the Mock Cambridge Exam that will be held soon. The real exam is given at the end of the year, sent from England, I guess. The mock test is really more important because of the timing. This one determines who does what after secondary school: University? Trade school? Teacher training for the lower schools? I am making up questions for the physics part of the exam. I have some of the previous ones so it shouldn't be too difficult to make the questions fair. It's a regional exam, so the local teachers make up the questions and we each will be correcting some. *Aarghhh!*

Thanks for sending the Sears Roebuck catalog, which I received today. New clothes look nice. I'm tired of my six skirts and eight blouses. I need to get some more made. Maybe I can use some of the pictures in the catalogue to inspire the seamstress here. There seem to be about three or four styles for dresses and skirts that they know how to sew. That's it. Two yards of material costs eighteen to twenty shillings. Add seven shillings to cut and sew, and you have a blouse for $3.80. A dress is fifteen shillings for the labor, about two dollars total.

Harriet

WEDNESDAY, JUNE 15, 1966

Dear All,

We are in the middle of midyear exams and the Mock Cambridge for the Form IV students. I am a proctor today. Sounds kind of medical, but it means I sit in front and keep an eye on everyone so they don't cheat or write letters. We teachers are mixed up among the schools so we don't cheat, either.

The Peace Corps inspector, who came yesterday with no warning, didn't like my biology class at all. He kept saying how I should have used "the tricks of the trade," but he didn't know any to suggest because he wasn't a biologist. Gad, he's as much a biologist as I am. I'm just learning the trade so how can I learn the tricks as well? I work harder learning my subject than anyone here does.

Only two of his criticisms were valid. I know I haven't corrected the exercise books this term. There's been no time. He blamed me for Anne's (Mrs. Birnie) mistakes, too. I'm carrying on exactly as she did. Of course, he looked at the books of the back-sitters. Naturally, they had spelling mistakes, but I always write the hard words on the board. It's the easy ones they miss. He suggested mimeos. I did hand out one, which I know they haven't read. Alternatively, he said they should be copying from a book, which is idiotic since they will have the textbook until the exam. What's the point? He said there is no color in their books. This isn't an art class! I wish we could do pretty pictures, but we don't have colored pencils or crayons. His evaluation had the same complaints I have, but he had no solutions and neither do I. The consensus among the teachers is that the inspectors are useless, though, so I feel better. Colored pencils, indeed.

You asked why we have a man for a cook. The men learn cooking as a trade so they can support their families. I doubt they would eat what they cook if they were invited. The women cook *ugali* (a stiff porridge) and the food they like for their families. They stay home and work on the *shambas* (farms) to raise the food they eat and take care of the kids. We now have a *shamba* girl and she's really getting the yard into shape. The men like the easy jobs and say the women are more energetic. I wonder what the women say about that.

The weather is cool now, almost sweater weather. The other night, Kay and I sat on our new steps built by our *shamba* girl. They make it easier to go down to the "front lawn" from the drive in front of the porch. We gazed upon the lake as the jasmine-laden breeze wafted past. How poetic. It was spoiled by cat-piss odor. The kittens born in our house now live in the bushes near the hall at school and come home on occasion, usually with diarrhea. Serves them right. If they'd eat the good food Kay puts out for them they would be healthier. The smell is disgusting. Four runny cats—*egad!*

We are down to eight staff. We should have fourteen. The girls have great gaps during the day when they have no classes, but it means I can give more homework.

It may be my Waterloo, but I've been having great fun teaching electricity. My book of demonstrations just says what to do. It doesn't explain the results or the point of the lesson. Well, that's the story of my life here. Make do with inadequate resources. It's better than nothing, which is what's going on in several subjects right now.

Harriet

MONDAY, JULY 4, 1966

Dear All,

I imagine today has been relaxing for you, since it is the Fourth of July. As for me, the past 30 hours have been action-packed. To start, July 2 (Saturday) was a holiday. On holidays, there is no work, no school, nothing planned for the girls. The girls feel they should be enjoying themselves because it is a holiday, but they aren't, because there is nothing to do. Boredom sets in and with it comes the "hab-dabs," as Dave Merchant calls it. They had some problems like this at his upper primary school last year. A girl with the "hab-dabs" either laughs or weeps uncontrollably, both unnerving. One girl starts up and others "catch" it.

Saturday night Betty and Dave were on duty. Several girls were affected, but calmed down after a while. Sunday it flared up again. By Sunday night Dave said the whole school was like a loony bin. Dave and Betty took a Land Rover full of students to the hospital. They said it was quite funny. Six girls with the "hab-dabs" were accompanied by seven friends. Some girls were laughing, some crying, others throwing themselves around, half out the windows, arms waving. Must have looked like a clown car. They all got sedatives at the hospital and came back to the school infirmary. As some girls were about to leave the infirmary, a leopard appeared and wandered around for a while. It was the third leopard sighting since I've come. Hysteria was at an all-time high after that. I don't think they were bored, anyway.

This morning, Kay and I went to settle our case with Juma. What with a change of magistrates and labor officers on vacation, it is our fourth time in court, and it's not over yet. The magistrate adjourned it to be settled later. Don't ask me why. I was furious; tears filled my eyes in frustration. We chewed out the court interpreter and his sidekick, good-humoredly, which, of course, did no good but made me feel better.

Back at school, the Chief Education Officer had just arrived, late. He was addressing the girls: therefore, no morning classes. At 2:45 pm, after the school laborers had left, someone spotted a grassfire, which eventually burned most of the grass around and between the dormitories. Apparently, only the laborers know how to put out such a fire. No one else seemed moved to do anything.

In the late afternoon, some of the American staff and friends had a nice barbecue on the beach to celebrate the Fourth of July. The sunset was fantastic. The sun was huge and red as it slipped into the lake behind the barges and the sailing dhows that drifted past. We broiled meat and sang songs until the full moon rose in magnificent splendor. Never let it be said that I lead a boring life.

Oh yes, two boys from my PC group came by on their way around East Africa to stay at Steve's house. They are teaching at Iringa, which is south of Dodoma, and they are on vacation now. I helped entertain them from five to nine last night. So, what with "hab-dabs," leopards, guests, courts, ministers, fires (bon and otherwise), it was a busy day.

Four new teachers arrived to replace the ones that have left. Two are Teachers for East Africa (TEA), the same program as Kay. They seem quite nice. The other two are Asians, who keep to themselves. Unfortunately, we are housed according to government protocol, the better the education, the better the house. The Asian teachers get the same kind of houses as the African teachers. I think ours are nicer, but the ones the Africans live in are more like what they are used to—a few rooms with a walled-in backyard area. I don't think they would complain if they had my house, since Mrs. Makonde seemed quite settled into one just like it when I first arrived.

Esther, our athletics star, won the long jump, and the 100 and 220-yard races at the national athletics meet in Dar last weekend. She could go to Jamaica for the Commonwealth games in August. Maybe she'll need a chaperone? I can't claim any responsibility for her efforts. She's been trained by another coach for several years.

The athletics group is doing fine. They are thinking about money for blouses, tennis shoes, and track shoes at $15 a pair.

Harriet

TUESDAY, JULY 18, 1966

Dear Family,

Our headmistress, Mrs. King'ori, has resigned. We are all behind her resignation as a protest, though she is the best headmistress we have had. I quite like her. It started when she was away, actually. Six girls were sent home by the acting headmistress at the start of the term. Three girls were brawling in a bar. Three others had stayed for several days in Mwanza with an "uncle." Mrs. King'ori backed up the action when she returned. When Mr. Sawe from the Ministry of Education came on July 4, he gave a great speech saying how lazy students would be sent home, etc. We were all thrilled.

As a background, some girls just don't belong here, but once a student is in secondary school, it is next to impossible to expel them except in cases of pregnancy. Some fathers would rather have their daughter under some other man's care and control than educated. They arrange a "vacation" for the girl with some promising groom and if she turns up pregnant, that's that.

Mrs. King'ori told us she was at a school where a newborn baby was found crying at the bottom of the pit latrine! It isn't so surprising. One of our girls, Mercy, a very sweet and quiet girl, didn't return at the beginning of the term because she had given birth. No one even knew she was pregnant. Full term. Some of the girls are quite chunky and have stout bellies. Mercy's loose blouses covered it all. We heard too late that Mercy's father was fed up paying her expenses. He made the little arrangement for her that solved his problem. I'm surprised she stayed as long as she did. Some teachers were suspicious, but we all want the girls to get as much education as possible, so we weren't going to blow the whistle on her.

So, Mrs. King'ori got a confidential letter from the Ministry telling her to readmit the six girls who had been sent home. They returned to school before the letter got here, and she refused to admit them. Mr. Sawe had signed the letter before he gave his speech here and didn't even mention it to her! On Saturday, Mrs. King'ori got a phone call from the Ministry of Education in Dar, saying she must readmit them. Since the ministry refused to back her actions, she resigned. This was the last of several such incidences for her, she says. Our second-in-command flatly refused to be headmistress. I don't blame her. So, today our head is Mr. Sangai, the regional education officer.

Sunday, a group of us teachers went to Dancing Table Rock for a picnic. It is the destination I often use when running with the athleticians. A huge mass of flat rock overlooks the valley and juts into the lake.

It was a nice day with a pleasant, cool breeze through the mid-afternoon.

Coming back, we somehow split into three groups. We got lost, as usual, but we all arrived back at the same time. The paths wander all over, like a cow might. You just have to have an idea where you are headed and take the one that seems right. It is difficult to judge distances on that plateau, yet, since the lake is on three sides, you can't get permanently lost. It's a big peninsula, with little bays all around. I have sore muscles, but it was fun.

This week, the Form IV students are taking the regional exams, the mock-Cambridge that will decide their futures. Right now they are taking biology. I think most will pass.

I tried to make the English muffins. I don't know how many ounces of dry yeast equal one cake of yeast, so I had to guess. We can only buy dried yeast, and my recipes are British. My technique will improve.

Harriet

TUESDAY, JULY 19, 1966

Dear Family,

Even though I just mailed a letter to you this morning, I'm writing another to answer the one I just received.

I'm delighted about the books. Send them immediately. Diana leaves at the beginning of August. Don't send the medical books. She didn't seem to think it was worth the expense. If it costs a massive amount, maybe you'd better send just the last two or three yearbooks.

About our court case with Juma: we went on the 16th for the final time, we thought. We were prepared but the inevitable happened. Juma, the prosecution's star witness, was not present. The magistrate told the "lawyer" that he's been wasting our time, and the case was struck from the record. The lawyer seems to want to reactivate it, but it is obvious that the magistrate is fed up with the whole thing, but not half as much as we are. I typed out a six-page defense with every detail. Now, Mr. Lawyer says he wants a copy. He could have told me before I typed it. I need all my carbon paper for my letters.

Today and tomorrow I'm correcting the regional biology tests. The girls didn't do too badly, no thanks to me. I did my best helping them review, though the material was all new to me, so I'm not sure how well I did at it. I didn't take biology in college. Anatomy and physiology were full of ruthless pre-meds.

I've been making things for demonstrations and sliced open my finger while cutting the ends off old dry cells to get the zinc disk to make a voltaic cell. Using the zinc disks, copper coins, and blotting paper, I can make something that costs $30 to buy.

Kay, Steve, Roger, who is Steve's housemate and a TEA, and I, may go to the Serengeti next weekend. Vacation begins August 5. I'm not sure whether I'll go. I'm rich, though, with about $300 in the Dar bank. That's good, because vacations are costly.

Harriet

MONDAY, JULY 24, 1966

Dear All,

I know this will stagger you, three letters in a week, but things are popping. We don't plan for things to happen in spurts. I'll see if I can pry next year's vacation schedule out of the powers that be. Right now, just who they are is the big question. I guess I must have mentioned Bertha King'ori, the headmistress, resigning. Well, the ministry refused to accept it. They fired her, instead. So now, the regional education officer is the head. They think we are going to strike to protest the readmission of the girls to the school.

All of us, students and staff, are really ticked off at this. It could come to a strike, but I doubt it. Someone from Dar is coming up by plane to soothe us. It is so political it reeks. I wonder why these girls, or more likely their fathers, have so much pull. We will write to the president himself, but I doubt if it will help. The teachers who are the most gung-ho to strike are the ones who leave in two weeks. What do they have to lose? I'm just playing it cool.

The new teachers are nice. One, an Asian, will live in town, so we won't see much of her, but the other two, both British, are quite lively. Some of the next ones to arrive are married. They will hang out with their spouses, so we will never see them.

The Mock Cambridge, the big exam, is over. The girls did not really shine, but in comparison to the other subjects they did quite well in biology—one of the few A's. I don't know about physics with chemistry. I am correcting that tomorrow. You can imagine the strain they were under with all the confusion here.

Well, I got my wish to see a rock hyrax up close. Freya brought one around to the front door in her mouth. I don't think she knew what to do with it. She's a golden retriever, but they don't eat their catches, so she just dropped it. I think it may have been sick because she is not a hunter, either. Big fat ticks covered all the exposed flesh around the eyes and ears, and the fur was full of tick-bumps. I have to dispose of it somehow. Maybe the leopard would like it.

Harriet

HARRIET AND ONE OF HER PETS, DOGGER.

CHAPTER FIVE

Second School Break

FRIDAY, AUGUST 11, 1966

Dear Family,

Goodness, a letter from each of you!

Saturday, all the girls left for home without incident. The last week was a complete loss; some girls didn't even attend classes. After they had gone, I spent 12 hours in the physics lab. Every piece of equipment is now clean, recorded, and in its proper place. The school opened three years ago, and this is the first complete inventory. I imagine pieces arrived in different deliveries in the first months and never got recorded all in one place. What a chore, but it's done.

Changes that have been made in our house:

1. A new dog, Dogger. She broke her leg two weeks ago and still has a bandage. Very intelligent and she is getting used to the three cats.

2. We finally have bookshelves for Kay's 20 feet of books. She is busy sorting them alphabetically by author. It looks so much nicer than my black, cardboard bookshelf (2 ½ x 3 feet) that the Peace Corps provides to all volunteers. It comes full of novels for our reading pleasure.

3. We have large, balloon-shaped Chinese lamp-shades in the living room. Better than the naked light bulbs that were dangling from the ceiling.

4. We have the material for some living room curtains.

5. We have a huge collage that Kay made, 59" x 75," for one wall. Not yet installed.

6. We have a leopard skull, waiting for the brain to drop out.

Most of those things, except the skull, are thanks to Kay. It is so nice having a TEA for a housemate. If I bought those things, someone would find out and reduce my living allowance. No danger of that. No money.

The skull is from the leopard shot on the grounds by the *askaris* (game wardens) from the game park. Someone in the next valley came out his back door to see why the chickens were squawking like crazy and saw the hind end of the leopard disappearing over the wall. It had already enjoyed several chicken dinners. The *askaris* said it had to be removed. Since they didn't have the trap available this time, they had to shoot it.

As the biology teacher, I got the skull with the bullet hole in it. Actually, the head without the pelt. Lucky me. We've had discussions with everyone on how to clean it. The best idea is to put it on top of an ant mound and let them do the job. It seems to be working.

The weather is getting quite warm. I'm very grateful that these houses are cool, often with a good breeze from the lake. If I could swim in the lake, I would certainly not ever leave this place. It is so perfect. My frustration at not swimming is extreme. I have to settle that issue somehow. Then I'll take up residence.

Well, as the British say, "Tah."

Harriet

FRIDAY, AUGUST 24, 1966

Dear Family,

The long pause between letters was due to the vacation, which (sigh) is over all too soon. I took a bus to Moshi, a town near Arusha on Thursday. It was a 15 1/2 hour ride. The next day, I rode another bus south to Korogwe where I searched for the girls' secondary school, not knowing if Anne Wiggins or Nancy O'Donnell would be there. Luckily they were. The Catholic sisters who run their school were on retreat, and Anne and Nancy were in charge. I spent the night with them.

Saturday, we three went by bus to the Kabuku Settlement Scheme to visit Cathy Bloom, the only member of our PCV group who is not a teacher.

Kabuku is a bit south of Korogwe. "Scheme" sounds shifty— some manager's idea. It's more like a cooperative. We met some Canadians on the bus who had climbed Kilimanjaro with Steve Sterk, the PCV from the boys' school next to Bwiru. He made it. News travels fast.

A great poster pinched from a University College bulletin board found its way into my luggage. "Youth and people of the world unite; defeat the U.S. imperialism and its running dogs." A real souvenir, so off the mark that it is humorous along with the "Book" of Chairman Mao sayings in Swahili. The bookseller didn't bat an eye when I bought it in Dar. Just another sale.

On the bus, we passed healthy fields of sisal that I assumed belonged to the settlement scheme. When Cathy picked us up at the highway, she said the big plants were owned by a Swiss company. Unfortunately, the bottom had just fallen out of the sisal market. The sisal plants at the settlement scheme are still tiny, so maybe the market will recover by the time they are ready to harvest.

Cathy is one of three white people at the project. She is a nurse in maternal and child healthcare. She helps the midwife and is learning about delivering babies. A German volunteer, Manfred, and Tom, an American Friends volunteer, are the other two whites. Tom plays the guitar well and sings Bob Dylan to the night sky. Cathy lives in one of the four villages of the settlement scheme, but will move to a concrete blockhouse in the center of the project when it is ready. She now lives in a mud hut and sleeps in a tent.

Anne and Stephanie could only stay one night and returned to their school the next day. I stayed three nights in a caravan, a big camper parked near Kathy's tent. It gets very hot during the day! I'm supposed to be working here since too much relaxation time is bad for us Peace Corps Volunteers. I caught three rats that lived in the thatch roof of Cathy's new house. Monday and Tuesday I puttered around tidying up while she took care of the pediatrics clinic, babies and all.

Wednesday we drove to Korogwe and picked up supplies, including whitewash. Thursday, we mixed the whitewash. Friday and Saturday we slapped it on the inside of one of the staff houses. While we were working, the water tanker arrived to fill the holding tank. Without ground water or wells, a big truck delivers a 55-gallon drum for all house water. Tom says he is going to build a shower for Cathy's new house by putting a tank on the roof and installing a hand pump to fill it. The sun will heat the water, and she will have hot running water. Makes you think twice about water use!

Cathy was a bit low while I was there. The settlement scheme was a good idea, but no money has been provided for anything even though people are arriving every day from areas where there was no land for them. It will be six years before the crop will be ready for harvest. Who knows what the price of sisal will be then?

I hope my visit helped cheer her up. The move to her new house should raise her spirits, but disorganization, rats, bugs, dirt, and poor food take their toll. Luckily, the two men are congenial. After seeing Cathy's situation you can take my complaints with a grain of salt. This counted as workdays for our PCV obligation.

I had quite an exciting trip getting home. I hitchhiked to Arusha to get the bus to Mwanza and had a chilling adventure. I arrived back home very late, but safe and sound.

We still have no headmistress. This could be an ungodly term discipline-wise.

Harriet

SUNDAY, AUGUST 28, 1966

Dear Carol,

I had to write a short version of my trip home from Cathy's for Mom and Pop, but here is the blow-by-blow account.

After visiting Cathy, I'd planned to take the Nairobi bus to Arusha. The 6:30 a.m. bus to Mwanza would get me home in plenty of time to prepare for the next term. Cathy dropped me off at the "bus stop," a large mango tree by the side of the unpaved road from Dar to Nairobi. I waved her off as she began the return trip to her clinic. Then, I waited.

The villagers waiting with me on the side of the road lifted cardboard suitcases, hoisted bundles on their heads, and disappeared down the spiderweb of trails into the bush.

What to do?

By the time the bus whizzed past, it was late afternoon and Cathy was long gone to her clinic, deep in the sisal plantation. There could have been more of a village beyond the road, where I could stay overnight. There would be no public accommodations and I was a stranger to that area, but there would be an offer of hospitality. That's the way it was in the bush. It would be awkward for villagers to take in a *mzungu*, (a white person) and uncomfortable for me. But it was a possibility.

Or I could stay where I was and wait. I had no blanket and only snacks for food, and no reason to think that tomorrow's bus would be less packed.

I really had to get to Arusha by morning. The next bus to Mwanza didn't leave for two days. It would not make a good impression for me to miss the first staff meeting with our new headmistress.

My anxiety increased. A lorry stopped down the road and picked up one of the stragglers. Hitchhiking in the U.S. is never a good idea, but in Tanzania few people can afford vehicles, and other Peace Corps volunteers I know hitchhike. Reluctantly, I realized hitchhiking was the only way to get to Arusha, provided another vehicle came along before nightfall.

Eventually, an aged but sturdy British Leyland stopped. The sturdy truck was like so many left from the colonial rule, battered khaki with a rounded engine hood and short slats around the flat bed. Behind the cab lay boxes, cases of beer, a new motor, sisal bags fat with some lumpy tubers, and cotton bags of flour. A bald spare tire sat on top of a greasy canvas tarp near the tailgate.

The driver's glistening ebony elbow hung out the open window.

I greeted him with my friendliest smile. *"Hujambo, Baba. Habari Gani?"* (Hello Father, how are you?)

"Nzuri, Mama." (Good, Mother or Ma'am)

"Nakwenda Arusha?" (Are you going to Arusha?) I asked hopefully.

I should have asked him about his family, but I was focused on my problem.

"Ndio, Mama," the driver said amiably. (Yes, Mother.)

He turned and mumbled something. A younger fellow hopped out, helped lift my pack into the back. Then he stood back to let me climb in the cab. I settled myself in the middle of the seat, tucked my skirt around my legs to give the stick shift free play and found a place for my dusty feet.

The question I should have asked the driver was when he expected to arrive in Arusha. The drive was only a few hours, so I might still have had time to rest before the morning bus. That's not quite the way it worked out.

The driver avoided the largest holes, but the washboards were a special trial of vibration and loud truck, bouncing body, noise. Conversation was difficult, but we managed some basics. Soon, we pulled up in front of a simple white, sun-dried brick structure with red trim and a corrugated tin roof. Colorful metal signs advertised Sportsman cigarettes and Bata Shoes. It was a *duka,* one of the little stores that sold cigarettes, plastic shoes, school supplies, greasy food, and snacks. For the thirsty, there was warm Coke, Orange Fanta or *pombe,* the local beer-like brew.

Without a word, the driver hopped down, slammed his door and went in, leaving me with the younger man in the cab. He was a kid, really, probably late teens, one of many who seemed to accompany people of importance, like my driver. Not filled out yet, but all smiles.

After an awkward pause, he asked, *"Jina lako nani?"* (What's your name?)

We exchanged names, family structures, and towns of origin. No, I wasn't married, nor did I have children. I was a teacher at Bwiru Girls' School in Mwanza. He was Mohammed from Same in northern Tanzania. The conversation didn't go much further. I was anxious to get moving and my Swahili was limited. We teachers were encouraged to speak English with the students to improve their language skills.

The driver was gone for quite a while. Possibly, if I flagged down another of the infrequent vehicles, my very generous, albeit absent, host might be offended, which could leave me without any ride. As I ruminated, he returned and we hit the road again.

Odd, I thought. Nothing had been added to the load nor did he take anything into the store. Then I caught a whiff of *pombe* on his breath. Ever optimistic, I thought, *OK, one (or two) for the road. Pombe can be rather weak. Not always, though.*

I revised my arrival time and slept.

When I awoke, we were stopping again. It was night. The driver was gone even longer. I feared we would not make Arusha by morning.

The third *duka* we stopped at around midnight was really jumping with loud music and shouts from inside. One or two men reeled out the door and stumbled into the dark.

For over an hour Mohammed and I waited in the cab. No other vehicles passed by. Maybe the driver really had abandoned us this time. At a point when both of us had our eyes open, I asked Mohammed, *"Dreva wapi?"* (Where is the driver?)

Mohammed grinned and showed me where the driver was. He poked his right forefinger into his left fist, in and out again, jerking his pelvis in case the other gesture was not clear.

I made a face that I hoped conveyed annoyance, yet I felt helpless. I was only a passenger. I couldn't very well be making demands, deny the man his pleasures.

But Mohammed repeated the gesture and added some. He pointed to me and then to himself, raised his eyebrows and grinned. This was punctuated with more finger and fist action. Only someone raised in a barrel could not understand this pantomime. I grimaced, shook my head and said, *"Hapana,"* (No) as if he'd just offered me a mango or Fanta.

Finally, the driver returned, not alone. His gait appeared steady. A tipsy bar patron grabbed hold of the passenger door handle and looked meaningfully at Mohammed. I was already as cozy with the driver as I intended to be. Mohammed got out. After some laughing and pointing at me, the new man squished into the seat. Mohammed climbed up onto his lap, still smiling, his head cramped against the roof.

My odds were going down. So far everyone had treated me respectfully: I was *mzungu,* a teacher. My dress was discreet, not inviting advances, but I was, after all, a woman. This kind man was offering me a service, one I'd asked him for, without even mention of a fee. But danger signals tingled. I wondered, *Could I expect him to put my needs above his own and his friends'?*

Any woman traveling alone anywhere needed to be alert. That's what I was. A woman. Alone. Alert. Ours was the only vehicle at the *duka.* If Plan B was hopping out next to a jumping beer joint on a lonely road in the middle of the night, it did not seem the wisest. My best chance to get to Arusha lay with this lorry.

The night was very long. I could only doze, lifting a sandy eyelid occasionally to look for anything that might indicate where we were. I hoped that whatever the driver did at the last stop included a nap and with luck, a cup of coffee. He seemed able to stay on the road and only weaved to avoid potholes. No animals showed up in the headlights for us to startle or hit, the greatest nocturnal danger. The few wild ungulate herds in the area were elsewhere that night. Domestic animals stayed in family enclosures after dark for protection against lions. Really, our only worries were potholes. And for me, time.

The sky finally began to lighten and with it my spirits rose. The calm rhythm of the waving savanna grasses surrounded us. We were making good time. I thought, *How silly of me to worry in the dark.*

The truck rolled to a stop. I tensed. The motor seemed to be running fine.

All of us got out. I watched warily as the driver opened the hood and stared at the motor. He stuck his hand in and pulled and poked at invisible things. Occasionally, the assistant went to the cab to rummage for a tool. The other passenger took a leak behind the lorry and wandered over to watch the driver. They seemed to be ignoring me.

Not a man-made structure in sight, not even a dusty path to indicate people lived nearby. From the clues I had sleepily gathered, a few signposts and village names, I thought we were at least fifty miles from Moshi and even further from Arusha. I squinted at my watch. It was 6 a.m. No hope for the bus to Mwanza or the staff meeting that day. I hated that thought, but things could be worse.

I hoped they wouldn't be.

A small rise in front of us glowed pink in the dawn. I turned to look back the way we had come, hoping for a cloud of dust. Mount Kilimanjaro framed a stand of flat-topped acacia trees. Fresh sun leaked around the tiny cap of snow on its peak—stunningly beautiful. My mind was on other things.

The driver and his helpers prodded and fiddled with the accursed truck, and didn't seem to like the results. I wanted to scream, but restrained myself. I still needed the ride. Instead, I gazed longingly down the road, trying to manifest another vehicle, anything to get to Arusha safely.

And lo! In a cloud of dust appeared a silver Mercedes Benz. Not bad for an apparition. It seemed astonishing, but was it? The car pulled up behind us with only one person in it, a dark and slender young man who stepped out. He stretched and shook out his light cotton shirt and slacks.

"Is there a problem, then? Can I be of any help?" He spoke in Swahili and then in English for my benefit.

"*Hapana. Nzuri.*" The lorry driver told him everything was fine.

I didn't hesitate. "It looks like they will be a while here. I wonder if you might be headed as far as Arusha."

"Certainly. I'd be delighted for the company. I've just come from Dar and it's been a very long drive. A little conversation would be very welcome."

His dusky complexion hinted at an East Indian origin, a good assumption since so many owned the stores in the country. They were known to be protective of their women and he seemed charming. I climbed in with relief.

Then I learned that he was Greek. Did it make a difference? Maybe. I didn't know, but stayed cautious.

More little houses, more cultivated fields. We zipped through Moshe and were approaching Arusha. We chatted the best two, night-drugged people can. Then he asked, "Would you like to come to my home and meet my mother and have something to eat? Perhaps a wash up and a nap? If you were up all night like me, I'm sure you are tired. It's just on the way into town."

I hesitated.

"Oh, I assure you, I'm truly asking you just to have some tea. I have some urgent business to do. I can send you on into town with my driver when you are ready."

I said yes. The bus for Mwanza had departed without me, so I had plenty of time. He also sounded as if he really wanted to go home. He had a driver, somewhere. That was reassuring.

A little old mother was in fact waiting for him. Short and bent, she wore a simple cotton dress with a loose full skirt. Wisps of gray hair escaped her head shawl to frame her lined face. She was delighted to meet me and graciously served some too-sweet fruit punch. Her son went off to take care of his business while we had a faltering conversation. She spoke very little English. I spoke no Greek. When I was sent off with the car and driver, I understood she bade me a fine journey.

The driver took me first to the bus station, where I saw unbelievably, the 6:30 a.m. bus to Mwanza still idling. Of course! They were rarely on schedule. We left at 9:30 a.m. Not caring when we might arrive in Mwanza, I slept for most of the trip. When we reached the outskirts of the town, it looked beautiful even in the dark.

At a late breakfast the next morning my housemate, Kay, greeted me with agitation. School was starting. We still did not have a headmistress.

It just didn't seem important.

Harriet

BWIRU STUDENTS RELAXING ON DANCING TABLE ROCK,
A GOOD WALK FROM THE SCHOOL.

CHAPTER SIX

Third School Term

TUESDAY, AUGUST 30, 1966

Dear Mom,

For the three days after I got back to Mwanza, the weather was cool and rainy, or overcast. I signed up for a Sunday excursion for Mwanza teachers to learn about the Sukuma. I hoped the sun would return for it.

The Sukuma are the largest tribe in Tanzania, and Mwanza is the center of their activities. We began our tour on a lovely sunny day in the Sukuma village where the chief lives, near the graves of past chiefs. Their presence is important to the tribe.

The Sukuma live in rural areas and in a good year, support themselves on *shambas* (farms) that have been in their families for generations. Their ancestors watch over them and tie them to their land. They grow rice, cassava, potatoes, and corn. We sometimes see their cattle in our yard. As early as the sixteenth century, the Sukuma chiefdoms began to consolidate and trade with Arabs from the coast. European explorers like Speke and Livingstone passed through the Mwanza area and must have visited with them. During the colonial era, the Sukuma struggled to maintain their identity and culture as their lands changed hands among the European communities. The Sukuma are united with the other Tanzanian tribes through their common language, Kiswahili. Tanzania is the only country that did not adopt the language of a colonial power as their national language, though the children learn English now.

Peter Hughes, a teacher in Bwiru, organized a tour to see the newly discovered rock art on the little islands near Mwanza. John Kesby, a social anthropologist, has been staying with us and was delighted to join the group. He's writing the history of a tribe around Kondoa District in Tanzania.

Twenty-seven teachers, seven from Bwiru, piled in to a small boat and we putted around the tiny islands near Mwanza. Peter eagerly hunted for the new artifacts and pointed them out for us. Some rock paintings resembled stick people. Others were spirals and circles. Bits of paint still were visible, but most looked like etched or chiseled rock that had weathered. We spent an hour or so poking in the brush and found a few new ones.

We ate our lunches on the only flat spot on all the islands. A few people took a swim, but not me. It was warm enough to consider a dip, but I know better. Maybe there aren't any schistosomes around an island offshore, but I'm not taking any chances. We got back at 5:30 p.m., sunburned and tired. John said he couldn't tell anything about the paintings.

I still don't know about our vacation dates for next year. We still have no headmistress. We might get another biology teacher, which would thrill me! I am teaching way too many classes to do all of them well. I will keep one biology class.

Mom, can you find a recipe for guacamole? Avocados are so cheap here I've learned to like them. Today, I got three for one shilling, just 14 cents. I finally perfected chocolate chip cookies! Hooray! Send a recipe for oat-meal and molasses cookies.

In Kabuku, Cathy warned me about *funzas*. They are tiny insects the size of small fleas that lay eggs under the skin next to the toe nail. I knew what to expect and found three in my little toe. At first, it looks like a gray, watery blister with a spot in the middle. She said I'd know when it was ripe. Following her directions, I opened the first one with a razor blade, careful not to break the egg sac, and teased out the little bag of fluid and eggs. It left a big hole in my toe, but the wound didn't get infected. It was quite enter-taining, like picking scabs, which I can't resist. I may have to go back for more. Haha.

Harriet

SUNDAY, SEPTEMBER 11, 1966

Dear Family,

I haven't received anything from you lately, but we have a clerk who is getting increasingly lazy and antagonistic. She may very well have lost one or more of your letters, maybe on purpose, and probably some of mine to you. This place is so disorganized, it's pitiful. I just teach and keep my head down.

I asked about our vacations for next year and was told that the staff will decide soon. Talking to the oth-ers, the mood today is to have two terms with a mid-year break. It is really the most logical since the girls are from all over the country and some live so far away they can't go home during a short break. If they did go home, as soon as they arrived they would have to turn around and come back. With three breaks, two of them are too short, besides, two trips home cost less money than three. Anyway, if you visit, come before the end of January or in June-July. I'll let you know definite dates when I know them.

Kay finally put her collage up on the wall. It looks quite nice. Since we still have no curtains, it makes the room seem less bare.

We have now four cats, no dog, and one rooster. The dog moved to the Merchants' (Dave and Betty) house next door, where she lived all day anyway. We were given another cat, very cute but not yet toilet trained. I bought the rooster for a biology class that is studying birds. It's so ugly and scrawny; the gender was a mystery to me. I wondered if we would get eggs. The wattle and comb are tiny, but Suleimani set me straight with a chuckle. I think he has his own way of knowing. Kay thinks the chicken scratching is homey. She wants some more to add to the menagerie. Just wait until I get my bush baby. All we need now is a cow. Why not?

Harriet

TUESDAY, SEPTEMBER 20, 1966

Dear Family,

The staff made a list of extra activities that we are doing, like sports, religion class, and so forth. Shirley and I have as many as all the rest of the staff together. I've started a folk singing group with the girls, not even on the list of possibles. Yea for PCVs!

We are supposed to get a pay cut, from 850 shillings ($121) to about 695 shillings(!) because some people were able to actually save money. Oh, no! Giving the same salary to everyone is asinine. Of course, some can save, but others are starving because each place is different. All the Peace Corps hostels in towns where we paid 7 shillings per night ($1) have been shut down, so we have to stay in hotels. The cheapest is 12 shillings a night, but most are 20 to 25 shillings.

Miss Triplow, the Swahili teacher, is the new temporary headmistress. She's very nice, fine at signing papers, but we need a strong hand at the wheel right now. She's not it. We volunteers and other overseas teachers don't qualify for the post, though I think a couple of them would do a bang-up job.

We staff are just getting organized for the term. I think the new physics-with-chemistry teacher arrived yesterday. Haven't seen her yet. The Canadians who arrived lack any kind of orientation and seem a bit unprepared. A new couple, the Coopers, live at the boys' school and Mrs. Cooper teaches here. Her husband spent a week fixing up their house and that of their cook. He even put in electricity to the cook's house and whitewashed his choo (as in "go")—the outhouse! Nice for the cook, but it pissed off the Bwiru Boys' School staff since he should have been teaching. Most of them started teaching within three days of arriving. When Winnie and I first arrived at Bwiru, we were teaching two days later.

The athletics girls make *maandazis* four nights a week here at my house. *Maandazis* are like flat doughnuts, heavier and without a hole; basically, fried dough, covered with sugar. The girls enjoy themselves, chatting and laughing in the kitchen, and they leave everything clean and tidy. *Maandazi* sales to the other girls will raise money for their athletic shoes. I buy the stuff on their shopping list; they reimburse me from their earnings. They do a good job budgeting and tracking the money, just like a regular business. They're also working on some plays and will charge a fee for that as well. It's great to see the students with some ambition amidst the rest of the chaos.

I'm off to see the Beatles movie, *Help!*

Harriet

FRIDAY, SEPTEMBER 30, 1966

Dear Family,

Please don't take that article in *Time* magazine (Sept 16, 1966, "Trials: The Peace Corps Murder Case") to be unbiased. Some Peace Corps volunteers here doubt Bill K's innocence. The story that his wife fell off the rock could be true—or did he push her? Could he have prevented her fall? An unhappy person could hesitate at the fatal moment. From what I hear, total rumor, the marriage was not as idyllic as some thought. But Bill is home free now—only he knows the truth.

We are definitely getting a salary cut to 635 shillings ($91) per month, prompted by the belief that some people are saving to go on vacation. So, it seems to me we should get a raise in vacation pay to 100 shillings ($14.30) a day, so we can at least stay in a hotel when we need to, but I'll bet we just get the pay cut. Anyway, unless you smuggle money to me, I won't be able to keep up with you when you're here.

The staff meeting today was useless. We can't agree on whether we are going to have two or three terms next year. Miss Triplow, our temporary head, won't decide. Last year, the first term started about January 15, so maybe you can think of that as you plan your visit. We did decide today to start an effective discipline system, which we need! One of the new teachers is a real organizer, and Kay is chief disciplinarian. Fur will fly.

All the girls got smallpox vaccinations today. We were told there was an outbreak somewhere nearby. I guess Dr. McHugh, our Peace Corps doc, will let us know if we need them.

Last night, just after Suleimani left, I heard a bang in the back. I thought it might be someone trying to get into the cook's house behind the kitchen. The moon was half full, so there was good light. It was about 7 p.m. Out the kitchen window, I saw a large animal sitting with its back to me about ten feet away. I thought it was a hyena, but as my eyes adjusted to the dark I realized it was a leopard. At this point, a leopard out my window doesn't bother me, but I called Kay because she'd never seen one outside a cage when it was caught here. We watched the leopard batting around an old wooden box at the corner of the building where Suleimani sits. Finally, the leopard wandered off.

We stayed at the window in case it returned. After a short period of quiet, one of our little cats tiptoed out from behind the box! I cracked the door and saw no leopard. Fast as I could, I ran out, snatched up the cat and rushed it inside. Once safe, we were curious where the leopard had gone. Out the front door, my powerful torch did not show anything unusual. Seeing nothing, we opened the French door and slowly, looking around, Kay and I crept to the front of the porch. To the right, there was nothing. I scanned to the front. Nothing. Then I moved slowly to the far left.

There was the leopard!

He was lying on a heap of dirt about 30 feet from us. He blinked at us, but didn't move, just stared. We yelled. He didn't seem to care. We tried to shoo it and yelled again. Nothing. We stared for a bit. I blinked.

Yikes! When I opened my eyes, it was gone! I didn't even see it flinch. It was there and then it wasn't.

Kay and I ran inside, terrified at how suddenly he disappeared. Safe behind the closed door, we started laughing at the absurdity of our actions. We must have looked like the Keystone Cops the way we raced each other for the door. Really, he could have run in our direction as quickly as he'd disappeared. I guess we didn't look tasty enough.

We stayed inside, but kept a watch out the metal and glass doors. After a while, the leopard sauntered around the corner of the house and stepped up onto the porch. He hung around for about an hour, making himself quite at home. We only have two cats now, so the leopard must've eaten the other three, including the two I liked best.

Christmas presents: label all packages used clothing. I would like two villager-type shirtwaist dresses size 14, two squeeze bottles or sticks of deodorant, drip dry print blouses, six bandido scarves for Kay, five black, fat point Lindy pens, one 8-ounce medium-rare steak from the Country Kitchen with fried onion rings, one pair of thongs from the farmers' market, one new bite plate, one genuine pine tree, a rose, and water to swim in. Haha.

Harriet

MONDAY, OCTOBER 10, 1966

Dear Family,

We are finally getting a halfway decent headmistress. She came to visit last week, tall and slender, early thirties maybe. In two more weeks she will return to take over for at least six months. She was head here several years ago and says it will take until June to straighten out the accounts. She wants the school to have three terms next year, but still no date has been set for the January start. Three terms means an April vacation. Well, best of luck with your plans to visit since I can be of little help.

Saturday I was on duty. In the middle of the morning, I was working in the staff room. Three girls ran in the door, bursting with excitement.

"A snake. A snake, Miss Dainsone. Come and see!"

One of the *shamba* boys told them there was a snake where he was working and they felt I should know since I'm the biology teacher. Surely, I would want to see it.

Well, of course I did.

I walked down to Mrs. Berry's old house, where the snake was still in the garden. It hadn't moved at all from when it was first found. I think it may have been sick, because they poked it and it just kind of cringed. I went back to the lab and looked it up in my snake book. OK, it was a puff adder, quite poisonous. After summers in southern Oregon, always alert for rattlesnakes, I knew what to do. After all, if my grandmother could dispatch a rattlesnake, I could take care of that puff adder.

I found a sturdy forked stick, long enough to keep me safe, and a *panga*, which has a two-foot-long heavy blade. I returned to the snake. The girls had done their job telling me about it and were off somewhere else so I was on my own, which I preferred. They get so excited at any wildlife—it was easier without an audience.

The snake was in the same spot. As I approached, the tail flicked a little. I used the stick to tease it out of its coil and pushed the fork behind the head to hold it firm. I cut off the head, and took head and body to the lab in a box. I was careful to avoid the fangs, even when it was dead. I skinned it. The skin is really beautiful, shades of brown with a chevron pattern on the back. I pinned it out and salted it for preservation. I hope I can bring it home. If I leave it here, the climate and bugs will destroy it quickly.

I've been wrapping and sending *kangas* to everyone for Christmas. Quite cheap, and I love how colorful they are. Their light fabric ships well. They cost six to eight shillings apiece to buy and 2 shillings to send by surface, which is $1.40 total, at the most.

All of the *World Books* arrived together and are in fine shape. I will get the head girl to write a thank you note to Mrs. Wood. My, those new yearbooks are really nice! We will put them to good use.

Harriet

THURSDAY, OCT. 13, 1966

Dear Mom and Carol,

Regarding your forthcoming trip: 220 shillings equals about $31—7 shillings to the dollar. I think "in season" for tourists is June to August. Do not plan a tight schedule. Anything can happen. I can be in Nairobi anytime. I am curious why you left Serengeti and Ngorongoro Crater off your tour list. They are the two biggest attractions besides Kilimanjaro.

Re staying here: I think that after all the sightseeing, you will be quite exhausted. You must stay here at least a week. Even two weeks would be fine. I insist you stay here at Bwiru. Beds may be improvised, but after sitting at the Mwanza Hotel for several hours today, I don't think you would like it there. Hot and busy. It is cooler here and more relaxing, scenic, congenial, entertaining. And, there's me. I'm here.

As far as disturbing my teaching, I have to be here almost a week before any teaching begins anyway to meet the girls, to clean out, have staff meetings, etc. I will be re-teaching all the material this term, so there is not much preparation. The girls don't work very hard for the first week of classes anyway. Stay as long as you like.

When you leave, you must go by Murchison Falls. That is one of the places on my must-see list, but I can see it later. Regarding transportation: bus by day from Nairobi to Arusha is the only decent one. It takes eight hours. If you do go to Dar, take the train. It is a leisurely, 1 3/4 day trip, and you see lots of countryside. I think First Class is about $15.

Otherwise, flying is the best way to travel. I haven't heard any complaints, although I don't know too many people who have flown. If you decide to go to Bukoba, you take a ferry, which I hear is quite pleasant. Another plan is to hire a car, not a bad price if you have enough people. There are many Volkswagen bus tours of the Serengeti from Arusha. Seranero Lodge, in the middle of the Serengeti, is quite lovely, according to people who have been there.

Whatever you do, do not feel hurried. December to January is the rainy season. The roads in most areas are muddy, but passable if you don't rush. Tie-ups happen, but I find that they are as worthwhile as the journey because just looking out the window is so fascinating. People coming and going, long discussions of what has happened and what will happen, none of which I understand, but fun to watch. If you gear yourself properly, traveling is a pleasure.

I know some volunteers who traveled by train through Sudan and got a boat down the Nile. It was January and cold but sunny, and they enjoyed it.

Today, we got rid of three of the girls who caused all the trouble last term. They were Form IV girls, obnoxious, who hadn't attended classes. Long story. Finally, a policeman had to come and drag one away. She left on the train for Dar. The other two live in Bukoba and missed their boat. They were put in jail, but later released. Kay had to handle it all and did very well. The wishy-washy Miss Triplow did nothing. It is 10 days until Miss Inkpen comes. I can't wait.

Harriet

WEDNESDAY, NOVEMBER 2, 1966

Dear Family,
Finally, the date is set —we return to school January 14. All staff has to be here for at least two weeks during the vacation. I am asking to make mine the first two, then I'll go to Kampala and get some dental work done and meander around Kenya and/or Uganda until you arrive, which I hope will be around New Year's.

Well! Miss Inkpen has come. And how! In the two days she has reigned, the school has been turned upside down. Classes have not changed, but that's about all. The rules are strict. Actually, not so strict, really, but quite so, considering we hardly had any rules.

We are getting a guard for the entrance road to keep out boys and other undesirables. I suspect they are also to keep the girls in, but no one has said that. The staff is being put to work doing what they should have been doing all along. This is no burden on me since I actually have been doing more than I needed to do. What else is there to do? The girls will do one day of *shamba* work, garden and grounds, each week, plus two activities in addition to their classes, and attend assembly every morning. (Last term we hardly had any assemblies.)

Things are beginning to roll. The girls are not happy with some things, but I think generally they will be pleased. The good students are willing to be neat and tidy, study etc., though it's hard for them to be the only ones who want to study. The miscreants are being pulled into line but fast.

Miss Inkpen said that the headmistresses are having a separate meeting in December to discuss girls' schools. Item number five on the agenda is Bwiru Girls' School. Ah, yes. Our fame has spread far and wide. She is really great. In her forties, maybe, and somewhat athletic. She and her husband have been in the school system for years, so she can't be fooled. The whip is cracking. Everyone is jumping. I love it.

Pop, you have trained me well. I finally got tools for the physics lab, i.e. soldering iron, hacksaw, a handsaw, a hand drill, et cetera. I've been working in my backyard building athletics equipment, sawing logs and iron beds for hurdles, and drilling holes for a high jump stand. Shirley's cook says I'm a *"fundi kabisa,"* which means a skilled workman, or more loosely, a jack-of-all-trades.

I'll send this off knowing that my chances of getting a letter tomorrow are high.

Harriet

SUNDAY, NOVEMBER 6, 1966

Dear Family,

Today has been quite nice. We have four more days of review before the holiday. No preparation, although quite tiring. Friday, I have eight periods to teach, the most possible. In a normal day I have five or six. After six periods of review, I was ready to climb the walls. A review session begins with my questions on the material and ends with questions by the students. That's the worst part. It goes something like this:

Student A: Please. What is suction pressure?

Me: Suction pressure is (whatever it is). Is that clear?

Student A: Yes, thank you.

Student B: Please. What is suction pressure?

Me: Were you listening? I said....

Student B: Thank you.

Student C: Please. What is suction pressure?

Me: (Livid) Ask A!

They just don't listen unless you speak directly to them. Except for that, I'm quite enjoying this week. No classes to prepare, no papers to grade.

The weather is very cooperative. It thunders at night. This morning, I slept late while it was raining, and then read.

This afternoon, Anita, a Canadian volunteer, helped me finish our gruesome job of killing 35 rats and cutting off their hind legs for this damned Cambridge examination. I have to get 70 hind legs of rats and 70 of frogs for the practical exams. I have no idea what the question will be, but if you ask me, it's a waste of animals.

I got my rats from the Bilharzia Research Center. If they were caught wild, I would say OK, let's do them in, but catching that many would have taken too much time. I hate to think what diseases they might have carried. I couldn't hire anyone to do the killing, or the girls would suspect what was coming. Anita teaches domestic science. Her field is nutrition. She worked in a lab for two years and has handled lots of rats. I suppose I could have killed them myself, but it would've been a strain. I'm an animal lover, you know. And I love frogs. I have to actually find ones for the exam myself. Even with the rain there aren't many around here and those are pretty small, so their legs are tiny. It hasn't been raining long enough for them to grow up, but I don't have any choice. I use chloroform to kill them, but it's the principle that counts. I don't like it.

Mrs. Singh, one of the new teachers, supposedly the biologist, should have done the killing. She's university trained, but she won't even touch our little kitten. She's a Sikh. I thought they were supposed to love animals, their grandfathers' spirits and all. That explains not wanting to kill rats, but why not pet a kitten?

Now, I have blisters from the scissors I was using on the rats and the *panga* (machete) from cutting brush. I love to cut down bushes and there are lots here. When it rains, the vegetation just leaps out of nowhere and takes over.

No letter from you, but letters get lost in the office, especially now. Great changes are being made, but the clerks are spiteful and you never can tell what they'll do. Vacation: I'll be here at school until about December 20, thence to Kampala and a vagabond until you come.

Harriet

TUESDAY, NOVEMBER 22, 1966

Dear All,

I just wrote my Christmas card to Granddaddy, and here I sit amidst stamp trimmings. An airmail letter costs five shillings in postage. I only had a bunch of small denomination stamps. I must say, the envelope is very colorful.

I really am up with the times. I just got finished sending *kangas* to all my friends for Christmas when that article came out in *Time,* but the material they were extolling is not a *kanga,* but *kitenge* cloth, a bit heavier cotton material from Java. Please set Portland straight on that point.

Kangas are very cheap, a dollar for about two yards of light cotton fabric made in China or Japan. Always of brilliant colors, *kangas* are worn by most women in the villages and some in town. One piece is around the waist. The other may attach a baby to Mom's back or contain a bundle of something to balance on the head. I've seen some wrapped loads that look really heavy, though there must be a limit. It is cotton, after all, and not very heavy either. Most bundles seem to be catch-alls with irregular bulges. I saw one on a woman's head the other day with an umbrella sticking out.

Each piece of fabric sold is actually two panels. It looks like they are made in bolts, then cut and folded for export. A sticker with the name of the company is slapped on, and it's ready for sale. Somewhere, the various pieces are mixed up so that a small vendor can buy a foot-tall stack of different patterns. They are not finished, but most vendors have a sewing machine to hem the edges. They usually have a wide border with something inside, often a central figure, pattern, or symbol with some Swahili words underneath.

If the women wear the *kangas* around their hips, the center pattern and the words hang on their butts. It's nice to know what it says. I have one that says *"Upate furaha wema na baraka,"* which means, "May you receive joy, goodness and blessing."

Another one says something about a rooster. I'll translate it before I step out in a crowd. Haha. Actually, I only wear mine in the house and for good reason. I haven't gotten the hang of the wrap and tuck.

Mine falls off at awkward moments. If it's the only piece of clothing, like a dressing gown, you wrap it up under the armpits and exhale to get a good tuck before rolling the ends under.

I have been studying the *kangas* on local women, many of whom are amply rotund. If you have an important message, I suggest you put it on *kangas* and give them away. A message wrapped around a pair of chubby cheeks walking down the road looks like a jumping billboard.

Every pattern for sale is loud by our standards. The shirt I sent Allen came from a bolt of fabric, not in rectangles. I've been trying to imagine him wearing it in Oregon. He will certainly be noticed, which he seems to like. The patterns are related to the tropics, brilliant birds and plants, and cloth. But which came first? Did the fabric manufacturers make cloth in tropical colors because they thought it would sell, which it did because there was no choice? Or did the muted colors not sell?

Now it looks like Kay and I will drive to Kampala around the December 17. Yes, there is a good dentist there. I think Anne Wiggins, a PCV in my group, will join me in Kampala. You can reach me by writing care of Peace Corps, Nairobi or Kampala.

I've finished grading my final exams. Now, I just have 1,001 forms to fill out for the girls' records. They are not just simple report cards, but a personality profile almost for the whole school. I should have taken notes, but who has time?

The Form IV students are almost finished with their Cambridge exams. After the biology exam, a few of the girls told me the frog legs were too little. They thought they were insects. I apologized, but I did my best. Tell the ministry. Tomorrow we start the grand cleanup and inventory. *Arghhh!* At least I won't have lesson plans and marking at night. *Yippee!*

Anita came storming into the staff room yesterday, mad at the ministry examiner who tested the girls on O levels in cookery. Anita has to leave the room when the test is administered, but said that when she entered the cookery room afterward, the examiner "was wild and came at me with fire in her eyes." Anita looked around and saw at each place a chocolate cake with white icing and, between the layers of the slices the examiner had cut, the girls had put thin slices of cheddar cheese!

The girls had been told to prepare a Victoria sandwich cake. So they did their best, and came up with what Anita found in the room. However, she realized that her first cooking lesson after arriving at the school was, in fact, the Victoria sandwich cake. It was listed in the syllabus for the Oxford Education Program for Colonial Education, but she didn't have a clue what it was, and there was no explanation. Being resourceful, she gave a lesson on sandwiches. Thus, the girls made a chocolate cake with cheddar cheese between layers.

Anita told the examiner that we called these layer cakes, and she shouldn't fail the girls because Anita herself didn't understand the outmoded English terms. She said that! The examiner eventually agreed that it wasn't the girls' fault. She didn't penalize them. And she admitted that the chocolate cake itself was excellent.

If only I had known. The cake the examiner wanted is something we get in the staff room for someone's birthday—white cake with jam, and sometimes whipped cream between the layers and powdered sugar on top. I just didn't know the name. It tastes all right, but I don't think jam belongs between layers of white cake. Some sandwich.

I wish I had someone to chew out for the frog legs' mess. At least Anita got it off her chest with a good rant.

I don't know if I told you, but Kay got a record player. It's a stereo and she has some classical, jazz, and popular music. The electric bill will go up, but it's worth it. My tape recorder still doesn't work very well. I can't get another cadmium battery for it so I just use what little juice I can get into it for a while. Just as well. I recorded all my favorite symphonies on one-hour tapes before I left home. If the symphony plays longer than an hour, the tape just runs out. I've listened to them so often now that I anticipate the abrupt ending. If I actually hear that piece again, I'll probably fall off my chair when the music keeps on playing.

Harriet

STUDENT TRANSPORT FROM THE SCHOOL INTO TOWN.

CHAPTER SEVEN

Third School Break

SATURDAY, NOVEMBER 26, 1966

Dear Carol,

The girls are off for home, and we have almost two months' break. Kay and I are staying here for a while before driving to Kampala, where she will visit friends and I will go to the Peace Corps doctor and dentist. Thence, to Nairobi to meet you and Mom for our tour.

I just got a letter that looks like it'd been crammed into a crack. The postmark is old, but it did arrive. Clothes for your visit: the weather now is warm with periodic violent rainstorms. Dress casual except for the plane. You'll be comfortable in light cottons. The only extra layer I wear is a sweater, but never all day. Moshi and Nairobi might be cool because they are higher in elevation, but you probably won't even need anything extra after England! Bring a bathing suit for pools in big cities. If you go to the coast, the weather will be hot and humid and the ocean will be warmer than the Oregon coast.

Blue jeans feel heavy in this climate. I cut off my only pair for shorts. I wear a pair of culottes for hiking in areas where I might encounter a village. The people don't think much of naked white female legs. Just bring a skirt or culottes that don't show dirt or dust, and you'll be set.

Because of the time available, I must confine myself to the Nairobi tours. Perhaps we could also get to Kampala on our way here. If you want to go to Zanzibar, you can go by train to Dar. If we can't fit in Serengeti while I'm with you, you can do that on your way to Nairobi.

Please try to find something like those felt stars we used to get at summer camp for honors. I want them for achievement levels in athletics. They should be washable, if possible. Look in the Girl Scout or Campfire Girl store.

To answer some of your questions: The spoon I sent is from Zanzibar: that's a clove on top. Our cat is "hairy preggers," according to Kay. That means she's pregnant again. The leopard ate her other kids. I've learned a whole new vocabulary from Kay.

Miss Inkpen said that if I took the boat from Bukoba on Friday, January 13, I could escort the girls coming from that area. I'll get my way paid plus an excuse for being late. Let me know if that's okay with you, so I can tell her.

Harriet

P.S. Things that are rare or expensive here to bring if you can: cans of B 'n' B button mushrooms, *nummy;* a box of straight pins, and one package of sewing needles; a good pair of medium-size pinking shears; one pair of Polaroid sunglasses; a triangular nylon hair net; Prell.

TUESDAY, NOVEMBER 29, 1966

Dear Mom and Carol,

This is to retract my last letter, since your plans seem underway. I am sorry you are not planning a trip to the Serengeti. Fanny says, "United Touring Company. Yes, it's just a run-of-the-mill thing and they take you around in zebra striped vans. You realize, of course, we won't be able to speak to you if you've ever been in a van like that."

So I'll have to be careful how any van is painted. She also says that the Hotel New Stanley is the most expensive in Nairobi. All the touring agencies send their clients there, naturally. The place is all right, but the food is horrible. Eat out. She gave suggestions. It's right in the middle of Nairobi, very European, and no Africans there except staff. Sad.

I'll try to come to the airport to meet you, 8 a.m., January 3. It's five to ten miles out of town, so I might meet you at the hotel.

I had Thanksgiving dinner with Jack McPhee, our Peace Corps rep here, and his family. Scrumptious! There were 20 Americans there. Not a very lively group, but the food was worth it.

Kay is in Dar now. She escorted the girls on the train and will return Thursday. Miss Jevons is back—the scourge of Bwiru!

By the way, Miss Inkpen is headmistress at Mtwara for a while, where that girl from Portland was posted. Boy, am I glad I'm not there. Isolated, hot, humid, a hellhole—the last post for government workers—the African equivalent of Siberia.

Harriet

TUESDAY, DECEMBER 13, 1966

Dear Mom and Carol,

Begin chloroquine phosphate .25 g (Aralin) for malaria right away. Take it every Sunday. Continue for six weeks after you leave here. It's what we take weekly as a prophylactic. The cure is a lot more of the same.

Anne Wiggins just came through from a tour of the Serengeti. She and some others rented a Land Rover and driver/guide for three days. They saw absolutely everything. It costs 2100 shillings ($300). The biggest problem is getting accommodations at Seranero, Ngorongoro, and Lake Manyara. For three people the vehicle would be cheaper.

Don't forget a charter plane flies from Seranero on MwanzAir, a light plane that will cost about $100 to charter.

Kay and I are driving to Kampala this weekend.

I've replanted my garden. The only problem is Freya loves hills. My garden is planted on little hills, thus she keeps sitting on my tiny veggies. So far, I have six carrots.

Harriet

SATURDAY, JANUARY 14, 1967

Dear Pop and Allen,

No problems finding Carol and Mom. We rested in Nairobi, hoping Mom's rebellious stomach would calm down. It didn't, so she stayed in the hotel while Carol and I took a three-day tour. We spent one night at Treetops, built in an enormous tree. The rooms are tiny, but bright lights illuminate the wild animals' watering hole. I didn't sleep much. Animals creep cautiously to the water all night: Cape Buffalo, various deer, wart hogs, a couple of lions, and more. During one of the few moments of precious sleep, someone knocked on the door because a leopard had peeked out of the brush. I missed it.

The Lake Nakuru flamingos were richly pink from eating the tiny shrimp that breed in that brackish lake. A guide told us that those we watched were last year's crop of babies. The mature adults were off raising their chicks on a northern lake. Rhinos, giraffes, and some huge vultures were there, feasting on a zebra carcass.

We spent the last night at the Mt. Kenya Safari Club where Crested Cranes roam the tailored lawn. They resemble our Great Blue Herons, with a bristly golden crown like the big comb a Spanish lady might use to hold on her mantilla, only sideways. Anyway, they were stunning. They must get fed because they are so tame, to a point. I tried to sneak up on them, but they kept just beyond my reach without effort.

When we returned to Nairobi, Mom felt better, so we have hired a car and driver to take us to Mwanza via the Serengeti.

Harriet

SATURDAY, JANUARY 21, 1967

Dear Pop and Allen,

Our trip from Arusha was great. Mom, Carol and I spent a day in the Ngorongoro Crater, an enormous flat plain spread out inside the steep crater walls. The animals can get in and out at certain places, but within they seem to be wandering in their own private reserve. We saw all the animals you might imagine and more! Elephants, zebras, hippos, rhinos, and lots of gazelles and their relatives.

We stopped at the *kraal* of a Masai family and looked hard at it from the outside. They build a fence of prickly shrubs around their domed stick-and-dung dwellings. They pen the cows and goats inside at night. Even though the rains haven't begun, the mud in the pen was deep from the pee and poop. By day, boys with long sticks drive the cows and goats to water at the edge of the crater.

Mom wanted to take a picture of the woman standing in front of the *kraal*, but when our driver told us how much she wanted, Mom decided to buy a slide. We found a good one at the lodge, which is on the rim of the crater and looks right down into it. The light play in the evening was magic. From the dining room the puffy white clouds danced across the sky. The herds grazed, moving around the floor of the crater, making it difficult to remember to eat. When Mom gets home, ask her what the crater's name is. (Ngorongoro) She can't say it. When she tries, she screws up her face and her lips get all twisted.

The last night we stayed at Seranero, which is right in the middle of the Serengeti and east of Ngorongoro. The outside of the guest bungalows look like the houses in my area, round with pointy grass roofs. Inside, our room was akin to a hotel with painted walls, beds, rugs, and a bathroom. Lying on the bed, you look up to the underside of the grass roof. I never saw anything crawl out, but heard some little rustlings. Geckos, little pale green lizards, live on the walls and squeak in tiny voices. They are our friends because they eat the mosquitoes. We ate outside under a shady roof and the food was wonderful. Suleimani is a good cook, but tourists are really fed well! We had a wonderful variety of food that I never see in Mwanza, and tons of meat, even some wild game.

More animals sighted: a leopard sleeping on a tree limb, which was a personal goal of mine to see.

On the drive to Mwanza, we bipped along the dusty road at a rapid pace. We were passing through flat plains with a few acacias when the driver slowed way down. I looked up to see some people gathered at the side of the road. As we got closer, I saw that there was something like a speed bump across the road. The driver managed to get over it by driving a little sideways, but he said they did that to catch unwary drivers. If a vehicle hits the bump going too fast, parts fly off. By the time the car turns around, the people have gathered up the parts to sell back to the driver. Pretty resourceful way out there.

Harriet

SUNDAY, JANUARY 29, 1967

Dear Pop,

Carol and Mom took off for Nairobi without a problem, though they were a bit surprised at the plane waiting on the runway for them, nose in the air, two propellers, and not looking too shiny. I expected Betty Grable to step off in her seams-down-the-back stockings. They bravely climbed aboard, so I hope the engines were in good shape, anyway.

They seemed to enjoy their visit. I showed them the places I frequent and even took them on a short hike up a hill behind my house to see the view. At the market in town, Carol wrinkled her nose at the flies on the chicken carcasses. I assured her I get there early to shop, when they are freshly killed. There really weren't that many; rank meat means more flies.

Suleimani was impressed that my mother, who must be at least his age, would come all the way here to see me. Ask Mom when she returns if he seemed older than her 50 plus years. He seemed pleased to make tea for her, and she was her charming self.

The weather cooperated, and the flowers were showy. The hibiscus at the end of the house was in full bloom, which Mom loved. I don't think she was impressed with my struggling garden, but the fence posts I pounded into the dirt to keep Freya out are sprouting leaves.

One day, Carol and I found our *shamba* boy in the kitchen washing dishes while Suleimani watched. After overcoming his surprise, Suleimani explained that he was training the other man so he could get a better job. I guess washing dishes pays better than whacking away at grass. He hasn't shown up lately.

A couple of days ago Miss Inkpen, our headmistress, heard a commotion in her backyard. She got to the window in time to see one of her beloved dachshunds trying to wriggle free from the mouth of a leopard. She yelled bloody murder, but it just ran faster with the dog screaming. Whenever she tells someone about losing her pet, she emphasizes how cheeky that leopard was to be out during the day.

Harriet

HARRIET AND HER SISTER CAROL AT THE BWIRU GIRLS' SCHOOL.
THEIR MOM SNAPPED THIS PHOTO.

STUDENTS STUDYING ON THE GROUNDS OF THE BWIRU GIRLS' SCHOOL.

CHAPTER EIGHT

Fourth School Term

WEDNESDAY, FEBRUARY 1, 1967

Dear Mom and Carol,

I hope you're enjoying Rome, and your feet are holding up.

Things are getting back to normal after the break. It was so nice having you here. Now, you can understand what's up when I write.

Miss Inkpen is getting over the loss of her beloved dachshund. She says her other one is very lonely. Hunters have been wandering around with their guns to no avail. That leopard is long gone. It has good taste, I think. A well-fed dachshund looks just like a juicy sausage.

I've been trying to resist stuffing myself with mangos now that I know the rash I get around my mouth is from the skins. Who would have thought that poison oak and mango skins contain the same irritating chemical?

Kay took her car into town for repairs today and rode back in a taxi. When she arrived, the driver demanded too much for the fare. She offered him the usual price, but he refused. Kay said, "Take it or leave it."

He left it and drove off, cursing. Now, she's scared he's going to return and chop her up. She went to Miss

Inkpen with her tail between her legs, and Miss Inkpen laughed. So much for Kay's fears of machete wielding, taxi drivers. Kay lived in northern Tanganyika with her family when the Mau Mau were chopping up settlers, so she has grounds for her fears.

Some miscellaneous answers: Kay's dog, Freya, is fine. She has lost lots of weight and looks much better. She was already pretty pudgy when she ate the molasses candy you sent me. I was hoping for some retribution, but she showed no signs of a stomachache.

The kittens are really wild and fun to watch, occasionally venturing outside. Daring little guys. Now, I must answer the heap of mail I received as a result of my August Christmas cards.

Harriet

WEDNESDAY, FEBRUARY 8, 1967

Dear Mom and Carol,

The banks in Tanzania were nationalized on Tuesday. I'm not sure what that means, but most banking ground to a halt, a big problem for savings account holders like me. I don't know if they've started to cash checks again, but I'm broke. I have no other way to get money because everything is deposited directly to my account.

Tanzania's President Julius Nyerere made an important policy speech Sunday in Arusha. It is still only available in Swahili, but from the comments I hear, he railed at the corruption that is stalling economic development. He praised the socialist model as a solution. Nyerere does not want people to believe money from the outside is the answer. If everyone works hard, the country will develop and become sustainable. All big companies will be nationalized, that sort of thing. We don't have any big companies in this area, but I like his ideas. He has some good ones. I hope they will work.

Remember the lake flies last year? They hatch when it rains about now and die in fluffy heaps under the lights. Anita, who teaches home ec, wasn't here for the hatch last year. This morning she went up to her cookery classroom. Some of the girls were looking out the window, which is unusual. A fishy stink hit her when she opened the door. Several giggling girls were standing next to one of the ovens, which held not a pie, but tiny lake fly patties. The piles of flies are mostly air so I imagine it would take one huge pile of flies to make one bitty patty.

The cooks had to be local girls. Last year, one of the girls told us with disgust, "Some people like to eat the lake flies." Not many of the girls wanted to try them this year either. I asked Anita if she tasted one. "Oh, no. Not me!" she laughed. "I just let them finish their baking project and then started the class."

I'm making rat cages from *debes* that I get from the school kitchen. *Debes* are the boxy, five-gallon aluminum cans that cooking oil comes in. I need to remove the bottoms. It's a very noisy process—lots of whacking, which reverberates in the aluminum sides. A machete is the norm here for such projects, so you pound in the tip at the edge and hammer it around until the bottom falls out. A giant can opener would be much quieter, but when in Rome...oh, yes, that's where you are.

Freya is in heat. All sorts of canine rapists are hanging around. Kay tries to keep her inside, but the dogs smell her and lurk, hoping. We talked about little diapers, but had trouble visualizing what to do with her tail. A determined suitor will not be deterred anyway. Vigilance is the only solution to protect her chastity!

The weather is quite cool and occasionally, rainy. I've replanted my garden. Wish me better luck this time. No leopard lately. Maybe the hunter did shoot him. What a waste of a gorgeous animal, I say.

Harriet

MONDAY, FEBRUARY 27

Dear Mom and Carol,

I love having a lab full of things to play with. I finally was able to do my favorite demonstration in biology today, one from my high school class. It was so cool I wanted to repeat it, but never had the equipment. You fill a large bell jar with water, cover it with a deep, flat-bottomed dish, and carefully invert the whole thing. Put an inch of water in the dish to seal the bell jar and insert a tube under the lip. Give the lecture about lung capacity. Hyperventilate and *blow* into the tube until your lungs are empty and your face is red. The water gushes out, leaving your air in the bell jar! Amazing. After the exhale, mark the water level on the bell jar. Invert again and measure how much water it takes to fill to that level. That's my lung capacity. Impressive.

I let a few of the girls measure their own lung capacity, but I don't think they had their hearts in it as I did.

Last night, students from Bwiru Boys' Secondary School came over for a play. They were loud and rowdy while the girls were presenting the play, so Miss Inkpen told them to leave. They refused. Their behavior was near riot stage, in her opinion, so she called the police. I thought it was just normal for them, but I wasn't responsible for the girls. The police came immediately and forced them out of the hall and back to their school. A few of the boys apologized, but most were still belligerent.

The running shoes arrived today. I cut out pieces for 12 blouses for the "athleticists"—that's what the girls in athletics call themselves, now. I guess "athletician" struck them too much like beautician, which is what I thought when they made it up. The girls can sew their blouses on the school sewing machines. Now, we will look "smart" when they compete, which is important to them. The shoes will help as well. They have been using flimsy canvas shoes or running barefoot and doing fine, but they risk injuries. We can buy the shoes here in Mwanza. Bata brand—cheap, but they still cost more than the plastic shoes most of the girls wear around school. And, very smart. That is important.

Our *shamba* girl uncovered some etchings on the rocks in our front yard. Most were masses of concentric circles, like the ones we saw on the islands last year with Peter Hughes. The edges are eroded. We can write it up and turn it into the right people and be famous! Ha.

Not much is happening. Three-and-a-half weeks to exams. I'm teaching mostly old stuff, so classes are easy. I'm going to escort the girls to Bukoba at the end of the term. It means a free boat trip. I prefer to think of it as a "lake cruise."

Harriet

SATURDAY, MARCH 25, 1967

Dear Mom and Pop,

I assume Mom is home by now. Soon we begin the term's most difficult week, the one after exams and before going home. We do have classes scheduled, but if the girls learn anything it's not because they tried—because they don't—and I don't blame them. Only the most motivated will pay any attention to me. Exams ended Tuesday, and Wednesday was a Muslim holiday. Thursday was a feeble day of classes because Friday and Monday are Christian holidays. Then we have six days of classes before the girls go home. I don't know who makes this up. Holding any class after exams is nuts.

The regional drama festival was held in town last week. Every secondary school in the region sent an entry. Kay directed our girls in *Antigone.* Ours was one of the three best plays, repeated on the last night! Kay has her quirks, but she certainly can get the girls to focus when she wants. Bwiru Boys' School won second place.

First place went to the Shinyanga Secondary School for a work produced by Andy Jackson, the chap who drove Kay and me to Murchison Falls. They did a Nigerian play, *The Trials of Brother Jero.* Jero is a fake prophet, cursed by women. It's the one day in the Brother's life when he is most severely tempted by women and comes close to his downfall. The character who almost does him in is a trader and Jero's creditor, who wants her money from him. Jero's character was played by a very tall boy who wore a wig to emphasize his height. He was a fine actor. The play was excellent.

I'm working on sisal handicrafts. Last year, I visited Cathy Bloom's work project where the settlement scheme planned to grow sisal commercially. We drove past rows and rows of the fat, leafed plants that look like huge artichokes with a spike on the tip of each four-foot leaf. Cathy said they were not, unfortunately, the plants the settlement scheme owned. The sisal is used in crafts, or to make twine or manila rope. You have to bash up the juicy leaf and tease the long, coarse fibers free from the pulp. I tried it on one leaf, and it's a lot of work.

Fortunately, I can buy hanks of the fiber at the market. Women around the lake craft mats, baskets, coasters, and other sisal items, so I thought I'd give it a try. I have a way to go before I can make my fortune this way. Still haven't perfected the technique of taming the sisal. I tried soaking it; there must be something else they do. I should ask one of the women who weaves, but most of the baskets in the market are from further east around the lake.

Kay and I had a long talk about the merits and necessity of birth control with Suleimani. He is a grandfather, very proud of his many offspring and their kids. He may be past procreation, but don't bet on it. Supporting the family is not a problem, since he's well paid by us, so the economic argument went nowhere. He is used to our strange ideas. He listens respectfully and then just lets them roll off.

The other night Kay was making a special dessert that needed whipped cream, a treat for some of our guests. She set Suleimani up with the bowl and the cream we saved from our milk. After she showed him what to do, he beat it for several minutes with a whisk. Kay kept an eye on him while she worked on the rest of the cake. She could see him looking her way for reassurance, or maybe he thought it was a joke. She encouraged him, but was getting worried. Eventually, it thickened to her great relief and Suleimani's delight. He likes learning new things, especially British cooking.

The weather now is great. Never too warm, often breezy. The lake is so tempting but no, no, no. *No swimming!*

Miss Inkpen goes on leave April 15. Her replacement, a nun who headed up a teacher training school, was supposed to arrive this week but hasn't yet. I hope that isn't an omen.

Charles and Bette Patterson, PCVs in my group, brought the Bukoba students down to present their play, and we all went for lunch during a break. When I go to Bukoba I'll stay with them during the layover day, so I'm glad for a chance to be hospitable.

Peter Hughes, the teacher who organized our island tour of rock art, came out on Wednesday to survey our rock art. He found new glyphs and was impressed with our collection, so this vacation I will dig about in the dirt for more treasures.

Harriet

Harriet and a student rest on rock mounds near the school.

CHAPTER NINE

Fourth School Break

SUNDAY, APRIL 9, 1967

Dear Mom,

Happy birthday to you tomorrow! Wow, 52 years!

At every break, the girls who live around Bukoba take a boat from Mwanza to get there. A teacher has to escort them. It was my turn this term. Bukoba is on the east side of Lake Victoria near the Ugandan border.

We shoved off at 11 a.m. The girls traveled third class while I was in second. I didn't know how I was supposed to supervise them from there, but that was the ticket I was given, so I leaned over the rail to see the girls on the deck below me. Really. They had no benches or chairs and no shade, and the sun was baking. One girl came up the stairs to the chain where a little sign dangled forbidding them to go further. She asked if I had any aspirin because they were getting headaches. I gave them what I had and they stayed on the deck. They could have gone below. I don't know what's down there, but since most people in third class hung out on the deck, maybe it was dark or stuffy. The girls make this trip at least three times a year when they go home from school at the end of the term, so they know how to cope.

My options were sitting at the snack bar or on some boxes on deck, but the deck surface was dirty. Some second-class passengers went up to the first class deck, but not me. I'm always good, you know.

After we watched Mwanza harbor fall off the edge of the lake, all we saw was water. As we approached Bukoba, the sinking sun lit up the large steeple of the new Catholic Church that dominates the skyline.

It was too dark for pictures when we tied up about 7 p.m. The girls who live in the town left for home as soon as we landed. The buses that take the others home leave between eight a.m. and four p.m., so we arrived too late for the rest of the girls to get transportation. My school had arranged for a Land Rover and driver to meet us. We were shuttled to the upper primary school a little way out of town. The kids in that school were already on holiday and so was the head teacher, where I was supposed to stay. I got the driver to take me to Ihungo Secondary School, where the Pattersons teach. They are in my PCV group. They were expecting me on Friday, but took me in anyway.

I was supposed to be with the girls all day Friday as they departed. I told the driver to come at seven, so I got up at 6:30. I was very restless that night for fear I wouldn't get up in time, but he didn't arrive until eight. *Arghh.* We swung by the upper primary school for the first load of girls and drove to where the buses depart. There is no station, just a bare lot. A few vendors sell greasy food, fruit, and warm bottled soft drinks. My job was to see that the girls didn't go off with their boyfriends, which is common. How could I know if they got on the right bus or even on a bus at all? I didn't know where they lived. Some guy hanging around saying he's someone's brother may just as well be a boyfriend. They all call themselves brothers and sisters, no blood relation involved. Maybe my authoritarian presence was supposed to keep them in line, but I doubt it had any effect.

I didn't want to twiddle my thumbs at the bus depot all day, so one of the local girls showed me around the town. We inspected every dusty shop, potholed street, and dented car, and we were through in an hour. After tea, she went home and I went to the inn to await Betty, who said she would take me out to their school after lunch.

I read from 12:30 to 4:15 when Betty arrived with one of the religious brothers from Ihungo, which is a Catholic school. We went to the beach where the brother took a lovely swim and Bette and I chatted. It was agonizing to just sit and watch him splash in the water. I asked him about bilharzia, but he swore Bukoba has much less than Mwanza. *Much less.* What does that mean? I didn't have a swimsuit, anyway.

I told the driver to pick me up at eight that evening so I could catch the overnight boat back to Mwanza. He came at seven. Maybe he needed a watch, or maybe he didn't have anywhere else to hang out. Betty said he had tea while we had some dinner. Tea at that hour means food as well. A British term.

On the return trip to Mwanza, I was in a second-class cabin, six metal bunks to a room, three high, with two ladies and five kids. A teenage boy walked in after we were all settled, and the boat was underway. He lay down on one of the kid's beds. I didn't know if he belonged or not, but no one made him leave.

I slept in my clothes on the top steel bunk, no pad or bedding. The cabin was quite stuffy. There might have been fresher air near the floor but I was mindful of Kay's experience. When she made the same trip she made the mistake of taking a lower bunk under two tiers of kids. In the night, she awoke to trickles of urine running over the sides of the bunks above her. The kids in my cabin were quiet. I got a better sleep than expected, arriving in Mwanza bright and early on Saturday.

Tomorrow we begin "office hours" until all chairs, books, and an assortment of school items are counted. The estimate is three days. I have no other plans for this short break except a biology field course here in Mwanza. The Serengeti trip I was going to do with the leftover girls who can't go home was rained out, the roads impassable. Some girls don't go home because of the distance. Some parents don't want to pay for them to come home. Happily, they'll all get to go home over the long Christmas break.

A few weeks ago, a man came around with a basket of carvings he had done in a light colored wood. Most didn't appeal, too ordinary and like what you can buy in the market. I did buy one of a guy sitting on a stump with a mug of *pombe,* the local brew, on his knees. I like to support local vendors, but thought his subjects were too macho. I asked if he would do a special one for me of a woman and child. I didn't really specify much more, or maybe I did, because we were speaking Swahili!

Today, he returned with my carving, a woman and child all right. I was thinking the child might be on her back, or by her side. Nope, she is nursing. That makes sense, but the breast she holds out to the child is five times the size of the other one. Rather grotesque. I bought it anyway, though I do hope if he does another that he will pay attention to proportions. Maybe he has never studied a breast for this purpose. Maybe he's a Picasso in disguise. I should have gotten his name before he becomes famous.

I have a small ebony carving from Dar. The Makonde carvings from the south coast are popular throughout Tanzania. Most are of witchy, strange, spirit sort of things. Mine looks like a boatload of happy drunks— four guys, one with a really funny mouth, like he's in a wind tunnel blowing his cheeks out. I think it's supposed to be a big laugh.

We were warned to check for black shoe polish over white wood if the vendor says something is made of ebony. Tanzania's ebony is a hardwood, so dense that it's the only kind of wood that does not float. The heartwood of the tree is black, but a log of ebony has a black core and a layer of white wood around it. Wood carvers are tempted to take economical shortcuts and include some white wood if it stretches their wood supply, and then polish it to match the black heartwood.

Harriet

SUNDAY, APRIL 16, 1967

Dear Family,

Many East Indians are leaving the country, even ones who have been here for generations. For years, they've owned and run small and large shops throughout Tanzania, but since Independence, they have been feeling a bit uncomfortable. They are resented by the Africans because they send money back to their extended families in India. And even though they have been here for so long, they keep to themselves.

The new resolution in the Arusha Declaration states that all businesses must be co-owned by an African. It's a lovely goal, but not many of them know how to run a business or possibly want to. I doubt the Indians will be thrilled to teach them how, anyway, since they hadn't asked for partners. Any Africans who worked in the stores were the sweepers and stockers. The Indian families who are staying are sending their children to school in India or Pakistan just in case things get rough.

When the banks were nationalized, some imports were restricted as well, something to do with the self-sufficiency theme. Thus, cement, road paint, and brown sugar are in short supply. I don't use much road paint, so I'm fine. However, this month our salaries were sent to the bank very late.

In spite of all the changes, Bwiru is quite peaceful. Mwanza is far from the center of things, so maybe more is happening in Dar or the Arusha area.

We had a barbecue by the lake for the eight girls who couldn't go home for vacation. If I can't swim in it, I can enjoy having a party on the shore, which is only about ten feet wide. Those little schistosomes can't crawl across the sand. About twelve other odd bods who haven't left town joined us as well. Wieners, hamburgers, marshmallows, guitars, and singing. Quite fun. About 9:15 that night, Anita told the girls she would take them home when they felt ready. They said, "We want to stay until the end," so I guess they enjoyed themselves.

Helen Inkpen left yesterday. The new Danish head-mistress, Sister Jacque Marie, doesn't speak English well, but is very good in Swahili. She is just settling in with another Dutch sister for company.

Last week, I fiddled about in the labs, cleaning and organizing until I got tired of it and went to help Kay and Anita inventory all the stores and ledgers. I don't mind counting things; it doesn't take much brainpower. Now, I have nothing to do until the term begins in two weeks. I don't think Kay is going anywhere either, though lots of the other teachers have left.

Yesterday, we had an influx of students from Makerere, the university in Kampala where Kay trained for a year. I thought them rather rude. They arrived not knowing a soul here and asked for a house. Not a bed, a house. *Egad!* How timid we were when we went to Tabora for the wedding. We should have been bold like them and demanded a house! I don't think I can do that.

Freya had puppies on Friday, eight coal-black little fuzzy things. She can't handle them all, so I killed three and might do one more. Not something I like to do but it had to be done. The father is either a German shepherd or a dachshund, the two who were the most ardent suitors.

Not much to write today.

Some miscellaneous news: I've found more rock paintings and carvings. One is quite indescribable; many loops and curls, and lots are concentric circles

We are at Anita's for a spot of tea with Tia Maria (coffee liquor). The purchase of the bottle was a great splurge, so it will last until I leave.

I've been writing for the Peace Corps magazine, articles on animals here, the rock art I found, and the biology field course. I'll send them to you if they are published. [None were.]

All of the rat babies died. Just mom and dad left. I think it was a vitamin deficiency. Perhaps we'll try again.

Mama cat gets spayed tomorrow. Hooray!

Harriet

WEDNESDAY, APRIL 19, 1967

Dear Carol,

Happy 28th Birthday, to you!

Monday, a friend of Kay's from Tabora Secondary School arrived with 48 boys and another fellow. They are on a geography club field trip to see the industries of Mwanza: Coca Cola bottling, soap making, and fishing. The boys sleep at the upper primary school and the two guys are staying in an empty house here. They have meals with us and are eating us out of house and home. Kay swears she'll never get married because men eat so much. We have such dainty appetites compared to them, truly.

Last night we all went to the Royal Circus of India. I was sorry so few people attended—perhaps 100-150, for a capacity of 1500 per show. At two shows a day and three on Saturday and Sunday, they pretty well milked Mwanza dry after only a few days. I was impressed anyway. It only had one ring, but nothing as bad as I'd expected. Some acts were excellent. They had six ligers, beautiful animals born from a female tiger crossed with a male lion.

I don't really know what to call the art in my front yard. Most are shallow indentations, like a finger drawing on sand, only it is rock. Maybe they are petroglyphs. I have found bits of paint in a few places. I wonder if something in the paint etched the rocks. That's why I call them etchings. I've been trying to make some kind of a direct impression of them. The rock is too coarse to make a rubbing, so I've tried chalk, paint, and wet paper with only mild success. I'm sure they are genuine and old. Look up *The Prehistory of Africa* by Sonja Cole, which I have. Read pp. 222 to 244, where notes refer to paintings of concentric circles and line drawings. I have numbered the areas in my yard from 1 to 30. I defined an area as an isolated drawing, or a group near enough together to possibly be one drawing. The scientist at work.

Harriet

Bwiru students in uniform on school grounds with Lake Victoria beyond.

CHAPTER TEN

Fifth School Term

WEDNESDAY, MAY 3, 1967

Dear Family,

Back at school after four days at Ukiruguru, an agricultural training center on the other side of town. About twenty teachers gathered to learn techniques for teaching field biology. For our first exercise we caught giant grasshoppers, abundant on the grounds, then killed them with chloroform and mounted them. You put the little body on its back on a corkboard and hold it while you use a very fine pin to pull one wing out to the side and pin it so the wing dries in that position.

The wing is really beautiful. I never paid attention before to this surprising feature of such a common insect. Once the wing has dried, you spear the body with a very fine pin. Mounted right side up for display, the wing is out on one side and the other tucked in. Such fun! We caught and mounted butterflies as well and pinned out both their wings. Pinned, suspended half-an-inch above the corkboard, they look like they're flying.

At the school I stayed with a couple just married in January. She's from New York and he is a Tanzanian who studied in the U.S. for six or seven years. He is quite Americanized and is now second in charge of Ukiruguru. She's never lived in a small town, but is adapting quickly. It is quite refreshing to meet a university-educated African. He has a self-confidence that's lacking in many of the schoolgirls and silent Ester, our Swahili teacher.

Esther took over teaching Swahili from Miss Triplow, another quiet Tanzanian. Esther is very small and creeps in and out of the staff room only when necessary, like for staff meetings. We volunteers are a rowdy bunch. I'm sure it intimidates her. She does speak some English, better than my Swahili. Her house is about as far from us as is possible and still be on the grounds. No wonder we hardly see her.

Many changes. Two new staff arrived during the vacation. We had two marriages. Kay's ex-boyfriend caused an emotional upheaval here when he visited. (That is an understatement.) I don't think the "ex" part is quite clear between them, especially on Kay's part.

Two days of teaching have worn me out. The general disorganization with a new headmistress is exhausting. Sister Jacques Marie is not up to speed yet, but should be soon. Thursday, I return to Ukiruguru to finish the field course.

Freya's pups are becoming more German shepherd every day. They lap up their water now and they cry, so we've put them in the old kitchen next to the carport.

Harriet

TUESDAY, MAY 9, 1967

Dear Family,

Now, I must settle down to the term. Mary Brimcombe, the new biology teacher, is very nice and quite enthusiastic, like Ann Birnie, the woman I replaced. Until now, the women teaching lower form biology were assigned the subject because someone had to take it, not because they knew or liked it. They were never enthusiastic.

The big news is that Kay is going to marry Steve Sterk, the guy in my group who teaches at the boys' school down the road. The wedding won't be soon. Kay leaves in August and Steve in December, when I do. I guess when her "ex" visited there was a lot more going on than I knew.

I think Kay is trying to convince herself that she wants to do this. People are saying, "They will be very good for each other," but what a reason to get married! They aren't exactly from the same mold. After the dust-up with her ex, Kay said, "Better to have a slave than to be one." Very Kay. I don't think Steve sees himself as a slave, but he is easy going, which will help.

Sister Jacques Marie let me read a confidential report on me written by Miss Inkpen in which Miss Inkpen recommended I stay another year or another tour of two years. Sister Jaques Marie would love me to stay. Though flattery works miracles, I do not feel drawn to extend my tour. I really do work hard, I'll admit, and I will be ready to move on.

Miss Jevons, who teaches typing and shorthand, is being her usual bitchy self. The Regional Education Officer is sick and tired of her. We heard she was shipped out of Dar to get rid of her. They can't send her any further away than Mwanza. Joan Freeman, a new PC volunteer teaching commercial subjects with Miss Jevons, is ready to quit. A few days ago, Joan was close to tears in the staff room because of something Miss Jevons said. Later, I overheard Miss Jevons tell Sister Jacques Marie that she thought she'd finally gotten through to Joan! What a sweet person! *Egad!*

After one more trial week here, Joan can ask for a transfer. I hope she doesn't but we all avoid Miss Jevons. I can't imagine having to work with her!

I got my vacation pay, $150 in American currency, so I can take it with me when I leave the country. In Cairo, you get 125% on your American money in exchange and more on the black market. Maybe I'll have to stop there.

Harriet

MONDAY, MAY 15, 1967

Dear Family,

I heard from Outward Bound just after I'd written asking if they had forgotten the application I sent over a year ago. They asked if I'm still available. Yippee! Sister Jacques Marie walked into the staff room as I was reading the letter. I asked her if I could go and reminded her that I'd have to leave school early. She said, "Oh, what is one week? Do not pass up these opportunities." I love her attitude.

When she heard that Ketty, our Danish volunteer, was marrying, she said, "Oh, how marvelous. Yes. I think everyone should get married. It is a very good thing."

It's all in a heavy Danish accent. What a kick. She is about 50, short, fat, and jolly. Another very young nun, maybe my age, lives with her. She doesn't teach. She just keeps Sister Jacques Marie company and tends their garden. Other sisters visit from around the area. Quite a social group, that sisterhood.

Housing is a bit tight right now. A new teacher arrived to replace Fanny, but Fanny hasn't left. Another teacher showed up whom we don't need, but she needs some place to stay while her future is decided by the Ministry of Education. Miss Jevons keeps pressing for a large house for herself. Fat chance. We all either share houses or live in the smaller ones up the hill. Mrs. Berry had a larger house for herself, but she was loved by all and had huge seniority. Miss Jevons may have arrived just as Mrs. Berry was leaving and got the idea that she could have her own house, too.

Joan has settled in and decided not to leave. I can't tell if her threat simmered Miss Jevons down. I doubt it. Miss Jevons may fall into the category of Brits who can't make it at home and "go out to the colonies" to be somebody. Only, she hasn't done very well at that even here. She's a little late since the colonies have become independent. Sad case.

Harriet

SUNDAY, MAY 21, 1967

Dear Carol,

I've been letting my hair grow. It's long enough to hook behind my ears. Kay decided it would look better if the back was shaped, so I let her work on it. Now it looks rather strange, long on the sides and short in back. When she finished with the cut, she mentioned in passing that she'd never cut hair and said what she really wanted to do was something like a pixie but hadn't realized that at first. I guess artists need to let their masterpieces emerge. When it is out of control, I have wings on both sides. I've taken to running my fingers through my hair to keep it in order. My hands get clean, anyway. No one has made any disparaging comments, so I guess it doesn't look too strange.

I've been accepted as an instructor at the Outward Bound Mountain School for the girls' session in August. Two of our girls may be going also. The climax of the training is to climb Mt. Kilimanjaro. Last night, I saw pictures some other climbers took of the same climb. All they could talk about was how cold they were, how they vomited, how exhausting it was, etc.

Mary Brimcome sat quietly listening to their stories. Afterward, she told me that she made it up "Kili" with no problem, smoking all the way. She must weigh under a hundred pounds. Mary said it really has little to do with physical fitness, but rather how the altitude affects you. One of our PCVs stationed right at the base of the mountain has tried several times. He was a football player, fit as anyone. He keeps trying, but he's never made it to the top, yet.

Kay is really smitten with Steve, but it can be a bit annoying. When they are here I feel like a fifth wheel, which I am, but since it's my house, too, I don't always want to be finding excuses to leave. Either Steve is trying to get Kay to help him choose a graduate school near one she likes, or Kay is reading passages out of various books supporting her "equal rights for females" theme. Kay is wrapped up in theories of marriage. I wonder how close to reality hers will be.

Last weekend was a bit much. They were here Saturday noon to Monday morning. I couldn't find enough excuses to stay away. So I laid down the law. Most of this weekend I've been blissfully alone.

Any time the temperature drops below 72 degrees, we complain, and today was chilly. There is no way to heat the house, so I bundled up in sweaters and slid into my sleeping bag on the couch. I read and played classical records on Kay's phonograph or gazed at the lake and listened to the rain. Toasty. Cozy. Bliss.

Two of Freya's puppies have been adopted, one by Anita and one by Joan and Lindsey Freeman. Now, three are left and Freya has become very protective. She nipped the school nurse last Sunday. Maybe she can count.

The lovebirds have returned from dinner, so I'll stop and get off the couch.

Harriet

TUESDAY, MAY 30, 1967

Dear Mom, Pop, and Carol,

The regional women's athletics meet was held last Saturday. We won, hooray! The girls practiced three times a week this term and it showed. They earned 48 points (five points for a first place, three for second, two for third and one for fourth).

Yeah, Bwiru Girls' SS Team!

They set two unofficial records. Naomi ran the 220 in 27.3 seconds; the best recorded in the last year was 29.5. My 880 girl ran it in 2 minutes 38 seconds. A legendary girl runner in Dar did it in 2 minutes 41 seconds. They've made her out to be "the best prospect for the national team." Ho ho! Going by the results in the paper, my girls alone could beat the composite team from the coastal region, supposedly so great because they have university coaches.

Rosary Girls' Secondary School is our big rival here in Mwanza. They have a good coach, but it's funny to see a nun in a flapping habit shouting at her girls—excuse me, coaching her girls. We jump and cheer together even though our teams are competing. During a break, she told me that in a few months the nuns will abandon their habits and dress in civilian clothes. All the nuns are on diets in preparation. What a hoot.

Last week the "Great" Mal Whitfield, an American Olympic gold winner in 1948 and 1952, holder of the world record in the 800 meter, came to Mwanza to coach sports clinics. My goodness, he does work hard. He coached 80 kids in all events for six days in town, 8:30 a.m. to 6 p.m. In the evenings, he showed sports movies in the schools.

Whitfield was not at his diplomatic best when he visited Bwiru. I couldn't be there when he arrived, so I arranged for someone else to host him until I could get there, about 20 minutes late. He was miffed because he had to start his own film. I offered to show the rest of the films, but he stomped out.

On Saturday, the Peace Corps doctor said to me, "I hear you were late for his film's last night. He was rather upset." *Humph!* He was lucky I came at all.

The girls learned a lot from him, so I forgive him. Now, we'll see if they will practice every day, as he told them to do. The best ones from this region go to the national games in September in Dar. A national team will compete in Kenya at the East African Games. The Olympics will be in Mexico City, but I doubt any of my girls will get that far. I'm not that good a coach.

An inspector is due from the Ministry of Education and we had to hand in our work schemes. I wonder what he'll think when he reads my Form III biology outline on reproduction, including contraception, venereal disease, heredity, and evolution. None of those are in the official syllabus.

I have started to exercise for Kilimanjaro. My thighs are very sore. At a fast walk I can climb the hill next to the lake in four minutes and jog/walk down in three. The paths are quite rough, so I can't really run up them, but it's up.

Harriet

TUESDAY, JUNE 13, 1967

Dear Carol and Family,

I started climbing rocks with Tabitha and Dorah. They are the two girls from Bwiru headed to the Outward Bound course with me in July. Only 80 girls from all of East Africa are accepted, so two from our school is great. I had no part in their selection and I quite like both of them. Today, we ran to Dancing Table Rock for the third time in a week. The first time we ran there and back by the shortest route, which is about twenty minutes each way. Next time, we tried a more challenging route and got lost. We had to climb up a pile of rocks to figure out where we were. From the top it all makes sense, but even though we might head off in the right direction, the paths still wander and we can get lost again.

Today, eleven girls joined me in this pioneering effort. Halfway there we split up; my half followed the long route and the others took yet another path. When my group arrived at Dancing Table Rock, we yelled out to locate the others. They emerged on a rock quite far away. After thrashing about in the brush, we finally got together just after six o'clock. The girls were worried about dinner, so we dashed back to school in 15 minutes on the straightest path.

I am getting used to the running and can keep ahead of most of the girls. They enjoy it, too, especially getting lost. A few days ago, we were finishing our run on a new path. As we approached the school, we came upon Anita, hiding behind a rock. Her Bwiru Girl Guides were "stalking" her, a type of tracking exercise.

When we passed the girls, they were having great fun but Anita was still in hiding when we left them all behind. I wonder if they get their badge if they don't find her.

At least six of my athletes will go to Dar, possibly more. They are chosen for the scores from the meets. I've been watching the results of regional competitions in the papers. The information is incomplete, but none have bettered our times and distances for the throwing events in practice and competition. I wonder if our stopwatches are synched. They should be in great shape if I can keep up the pace, practice with them on the field three times a week, and run two to three times more. I shall come home an Amazon (haha!). Perhaps I'll try out for the Olympic team, maybe in rock climbing or double kayak.

I'm really doing exciting things in biology now, using an experiential learning textbook I got in my field biology class, as opposed to the one from the Ministry of Education. The model to date has been rote learning. I talk. They listen. They write down what I've said on a test. It is not very exciting for any of us, so I'm trying the new method with my Form II classes. I know it won't teach them what is asked in the Cambridge exam, but they'll have time to catch up. Until then, they might learn something valuable beyond memorizing notes.

For example, I have the class surveying grasses and plants in different areas, mostly on the playing field. They throw a hoop, count the number of species inside it and compare notes. On the first day, all the girls did as told. They returned to the lab with their data, gave it to me, and wanted to know if they had the right answer. The book has some exercises on how to deal with the data, but there is no "right" answer. It was quite a foreign concept for them, to do all that work and not have "an answer." Who knows what doors this twist might open for them?

The Form III students are studying evolution. To get their attention, I asked Anita to introduce the units on reproduction, heredity, and genetics. As a devout Catholic, she has more credibility than I do in that field. If I tried to just launch into the topic, the girls would turn me off because: a) I'm not religious and b) I'm a scientist, which also means not religious. But I've been reading the Bible and can quote it better than they can. When I do, they clam up.

The girls are required to take a *dini* (religion) period on Fridays. I'm sure they bring up my radical ideas about evolution with their *dini* teachers. When I asked if they believed me, one of them said with a sad face, "Now, Miss Dainsone, our *dini* teachers tell us that evolution does not happen. You tell us that it does. If we believe our *dini* teachers we may miss a question on the Cambridge, but if we believe you, we will not go to heaven after we die." A dilemma, indeed.

Even Anita had difficulty overcoming this resistance. I'm fine with it as long as they give the best answer in the Cambridge Exam.

We've had some staff changes. Miss Jevons finally left, to be replaced by a Tanzanian man and his family. They will take a house for themselves. The ministry wants Ken and Kathy Simpson to move into town. Kathy teaches here and Ken is a town engineer. Kathy rates a house, but they don't like Ken on the grounds— but they will assign a man to teach the girls? It's nuts.

Marilyn and Sid Cooper, who were here for two terms, were transferred to the teacher training college on the other side of town, where they are so overstaffed that one teacher only has six periods a week. Another only teaches physical education! The ministry seems to have trouble placing couples. Grumble.

The Outward Bound course is July 31 to August 23. The address is Loitokitok, Kenya, on the north side of the mountain.

Lindsay Freeman, who is Jewish, took three days off to listen to the BBC reporting on the Israeli-Arab conflict and gives us updates. Will they ever stop fighting?

Sister Jacque Marie is jolly, willing, and eager, but a rather scatterbrained administrator. She lost the instructions for the Cambridge biology practical, which I need so I know what to prepare. It's confidential and I haven't read it yet. I do hope they show up.

Harriet

THURSDAY, JUNE 22, 1967

Dear Carol, Mom, Pop, and Al,

A memo from the Peace Corps arrived. The new policy from the Ministry of Education is to not allow us to extend our contracts. I happened to mention this within earshot of Sister Jacques Marie. She turned around and said, "Oh, I'm sure we can do something about that."

I was a bit taken aback, since I wasn't planning to stay anyway. Later, she told me she had some friends who could fix everything. But now there is more news. Recently, a committee of TANU, [Tanzania African National Union] the national party, recommended, among other things, the immediate removal of American Peace Corps. So, I may be home sooner than you think.

The Peace Corps will pay for my plane ticket at the end of my service from here to Portland. It has unlimited stops and no time limit. I can use 150% of the miles from here to home. Pretty generous. Since I'm halfway around the world from Oregon, I've decided to go east and dawdle home. If I come across a place I like, I might stay for a year or so. Most big cities have English-speaking secondary schools. Science teachers, especially ones who can do all sciences like me, ahem, are always needed. One year is not so long in a new place and the local pay rates can't be worse than Peace Corps. I am not enthralled with teaching, but it's a practical job.

Miscellaneous news: We had another beach party Saturday.

The dogs have demolished our garden.

The cats have demolished my letters.

Kay will leave in about a month.

Carol's letter took 5 days to get here. Pop's took 13 days.

And now, my brain is empty.

Harriet

WEDNESDAY, JUNE 28, 1967

Dear Mom, Carol, Pop, and Al,

The fiancé of one of our teachers works for the Ministry of Education and made an official visit recently. I was doing a triple class on electricity, not one of my most outstanding lessons. I thought he was just going to inspect maths, so I was quite unprepared for him to sit in on my classes, but he said it was very good. He liked the relaxed atmosphere. I can tell you, three solid classes of physics about relaxes me to sleep! The inspector who came with him was not so nice to the teachers he inspected.

Last weekend, some men drowned off our beach. The story is that six or seven men went out in a tiny metal motorboat to shoot birds on the rock islets. The boat overturned and sank, and the current carried them away. One Asian and one African made it back to shore. An Asian body was recovered after an hour, but I haven't heard about the rest, assumed drowned. The men who drowned were married. Shops closed and streams of people came out to watch the rescue operations. I hope all the bodies have been recovered. I don't fancy finding one on the beach.

I just chased away a hyena from our front porch. When Freya eats out there, she leaves bones all over and the hyenas know it. She really raises a ruckus at night when we forget to collect the leftover tidbits, but the hyenas pay no attention to her. They know she can't do anything but bark from inside. When they've had a good gnaw, they amble off. I fear she'll get ulcers.

We only have one puppy left, the cutest one. Anita has one. She and the puppy will move in with me after Kay leaves.

After Outward Bound, I hope to meet up with the athletics girls and chaperone them at the meet in Dar—but I don't know if that will work out.

Harriet

SATURDAY, JULY 8, 1967

Dear All,

Happy birthday, Pop!

Fourth of July was uneventful here, but the seventh was Saba Saba, Tanzanian Independence Day. Actually, it commemorates the founding of TANU, the national party, in 1954. Tanganyika and Zanzibar were both under UN trusteeships administered by the United Kingdom. Tanganyika became independent in 1961, Zanzibar in 1963, and they joined to form Tanzania in 1964. So they are still working things out.

On the sixth, I took a group of Bwiru girls to a competition of singing and dancing at the fairgrounds. After they performed, some of us went to see the exhibits at the stadium. The booths, decorated with flapping fabric, held lots of local crafts, baskets, and carvings, like a country fair.

Several stages were set up for dancing demonstrations and I joined a few of our girls to watch. Most dancers were Sukuma, the largest tribal group in Tanzania who cluster in this area. The new dances were all about self-help and the turn to the socialist model of economic development. The younger dancers mimed using hoes to plant and harvest crops. Everyone is supposed to work hard. If they do, then everything will be fine.

A few old men did traditional dances. Most wore their street clothes, but there were a few chicken feather bonnets and beads. The most exciting group used a defanged cobra to "revive" some men who, the girls said with a laugh, had had their heads cut off. I don't know why, but they thought it was hysterical. The old man with a peg leg who begs in front of the hotel was helping the dancers.

People get dressed up for this national celebration. For women, formal dress is a two-piece outfit with a relatively tight skirt and top of the same material—cloth from bolts, bright and busy, but not rectangular. A broad ruffle flares out at the waist.

After a while, some other Europeans arrived and I realized how my white face must stand out. When

I returned to the competition stage, the awards were being called. Our students received first prize in singing and third in dancing. Hooray for Bwiru girls! They created the performances themselves. Some of the older girls are very good organizers and made everyone practice. It paid off for them. I was pleased to see them be recognized for something good after the school's recent infamy.

I still run with the girls to Dancing Table Rock on Sunday, Tuesday, and Thursday. Last Saturday, we competed in the last track meet before the competition in Dar. I think five to eight of my girls will be on the Mwanza regional team. This week, we rested for the holidays. Then we start serious athletics practice again on Sunday.

At the meet Saturday, I met some of the students in the Crossroads Africa group, the volunteer program I did in Malawi while I was in college. Their project is in Nyegezi, not too far out of town. They're shocked that Mwanza has no hamburgers in the greasy spoon! (Why would there be? It's run by East Indians). The Crossroaders said they came to all the Saba Saba events. Do you remember that we participated in the Malawi Independence celebrations? We rode to town on a lorry bed, dressed in our finest. National holidays are a good way for the Crossroaders to see the community, learn some history, and meet the people.

I can see tension developing in their group. When they arrived, they said no one knew what to do with them at their site. Their make-work projects don't seem important to them. The dormitory we built had a foundation and used lots of bricks. An experienced mason was assigned to our project to teach us how to lay bricks and to rip out our mistakes. Too bad no one asked me for a project for these guys. There are lots of things they could have done around our school.

The Crossroaders ate with the students where they were living at an upper primary school, so everyone thinks they are "starry eyed idealists!" What next? Crossroads is on a tight budget. They want the students to have the most intense experience possible. Of course, they ate with the students. People here don't realize that Crossroads is a great tour of Africa.

When I was in Malawi we met some Peace Corps volunteers and they seemed so mature and responsible, doing such an important job. Now, it's funny to be on the other end of that formula. I went on the program in college to check things out in case I decided to apply for the Peace Corps. My question to myself was: *Can I go to Africa and return?*

I did, and here I am again. It must have worked.

Freya leads the pack of dogs that wander around here. I watched seven of them swim the lake today. They were having so much fun, I was jealous. I'd love to be a dog. I guess it would be hard to tell if a dog got bilharzia, they scratch and sleep so much anyway. And who is going to tell them they can't swim in the lake?

One of the girls is cross-stitching a Greek key design on a tablecloth and napkins for me. That will cost me 21 shillings ($3) in labor. Pretty good price.

Harriet

TUESDAY, JULY 18, 1967

Dear All,

Last weekend, Anita and I stayed with Kathy and Ken Simpson who now live in town. Their house is large but has a strange design, not the standard box like ours. It was a nice change of scene anyway.

This weekend I spent most of Friday and Saturday making batiks. You wax a pattern onto cloth and dye it. The wax resists the dye, so when you iron it off, a pattern emerges from the non-waxed areas. It's fun, but I got so much flack about my lack of artistic talents that my enthusiasm faded. They were right. I just like to try things out.

On our Dancing Table Rock run Sunday, I let one of the girls lead the return trip. She loves fruit, so we wandered from tree to tree, eating as we went. We weren't watching where we were going and came to a very steep drop-off, eight or ten feet. Three of us climbed down, but the other two froze up on top— too steep for them. They laughed hysterically, nervous I think. Eventually, we talked them down and we finished the run.

Monday, President Nyerere came to town for a meeting with teachers. We three Peace Corps volunteers from Bwiru rode to town on the lorry, a flatbed truck with short sides, as a demonstration of something that evades me now. There weren't enough cars to take everyone, anyway. And, a miracle, he arrived on time! Everything was in Swahili and I could understand some of it. Nyerere is a very good speaker. He said the Peace Corps was doing a fine job, but "some people in Dar don't think so." I hope that means I'll stay to the end of my tour.

That evening, Marilyn Cooper was hosting a dinner for the Crossroaders and invited me to join them. They say they feel restricted, afraid to walk where they would like. Their leader wants them to be careful when they wander around the village. Trouble could erupt if they mosey into someone else's property without an invitation, or take a photo without getting permission. I don't know how sensitive they are to the local culture, but common courtesy helps. I wonder if we were intrusive in

Malawi when I was a Crossroader. I felt that way some-times. I did sneak a few photos when I was reluctant to ask permission.

Exams have begun for Forms I, II and III students. Since I organized them, everything is going smoothly. Sister Jacques Marie didn't even know they started today. I worry she will be in deep trouble when Anita and Kathy and I leave. We have been doing a lot of her work and I don't even think she is aware of it.

Essentially, the term is over even though the girls haven't left.

Tomorrow I find out from the regional athletics com-mittee who will go to Dar for the national meet. Right now, I just don't care because only two or three prac-tice regularly. They don't seem to remember that they are supposed to practice events three days a week and run the other three days. I am on the field five days a week, usually working with half of them while the oth-ers run. One day a week they are all supposed to be on the field, but they aren't. Pretty frustrating after such a good showing at the last meet.

Kay is having trouble getting her boat ticket home because of the problems near the Suez Canal. Now she doesn't leave until August 19. [After the Arab-Israeli War, called the Six Day War, an Egyptian blockade closed the Suez Canal.]

I go to Loitokitok soon for the Outward Bound course. The school is located on the north side of Kilimanjaro, so I take a bus west to Arusha first and then to Loitokitok, which is only a wide spot in the road. I leave a few days before the end of the term, so Anita will be able to move in before Kay leaves. I told her to take Kay's big room since I only have another term here.

I'll miss Kay. We got along well together, though I will with Anita, I'm sure. I'll especially miss Kay's stuff. Anita and I together don't have many things, so this house may echo a bit.

Harriet

WEDNESDAY, JULY 26, 1967

Dear Carol, Al, Mom, and Pop,

I'm exhausted. I've been grading Biology Form IV students' regional exams and my own exams that I gave the lower form students. Now, all the bloody forms to fill out. Bureaucracy!

Last Friday, a rumor went around that there was to be no vacation at all. New policy from somewhere. "Secondary students are now required to help with the census." Major panic. We (staff) were up in arms. First, they shut the girls in with guards at the gate. Then, they tell them to go out into the villages to count people. Madness. Today, the word is that the students can go home. I'm leaving tomorrow for the Outward Bound course and once I get on that bus, I'm gone. Bwiru is on its own.

The results for the Mock Cambridge physics-with-chemistry exam were disappointing, but students had bad luck. We, the local committee, told the examiner to have them choose five questions out of fifteen. He had them choose five out of ten. They were the most difficult I've seen, far more difficult than the Cambridge itself. This exam is more important for their futures. I don't even know why they have to take the Cambridge in December because by then, they know if they will be going on for more education or not.

Kay's replacement, Judith, who lives on the hill next to Anita, saw the leopard last night about 6:30 p.m. He walked across her front steps. Cheeky bugger, as Kay would say.

We just packed up Kay's refrigerator to go to Fanny's. Anita will bring hers with her.

My next letter will be from Loitokitok. Outward Bound here I come!!

Harriet

HARRIET ON THE SLOPES OF MT. KILIMANJARO.

CHAPTER ELEVEN

Fifth School Break
OUTWARD BOUND MOUNTAIN SCHOOL
AND CLIMBING MT. KILIMANJARO

SATURDAY, AUGUST 5, 1967

Dear Family,

Fifteen hours out of Mwanza, the rattling bus made its final turn into Arusha. A solitary, snow-capped peak swung into view— Mt. Kilimanjaro. My heart flipped. I was on my way to join the Outward Bound Mountain School (OBMS) and to climb the legendary peak that loomed enormous in the sky before me. By assisting in the OBMS program for girls, I would view East Africa from a place reached only by a privileged few.

The next morning, I joined an effervescent group of young women to board the bus for Loitokitok on the southern Kenyan border. Every student had been chosen by her school as a potential leader. Many knew each other and they were wild with excitement. I wondered, *Would I be working with any of them? Could I do it?* For six weeks, I had gone on runs with my athletics team that included the two students from my school who would join me soon. Was it enough?

Outward Bound was founded by the British during World War II, when German submarines were sinking an appalling number of British ships. The British had learned that older, experienced men survived the days and sometimes weeks in the small life rafts better than the younger ones, who often gave up hope of rescue and died. When the school challenged young sailors with problem solving and survival simulations, more of them were able to cope with sinking, which many were destined to experience. After the war, the successful program added leadership training and reinvented itself as a program for civilians.

On our bumpy ride around the mountain we passed bright green coffee plantations high on the slopes. Close to the road, villagers tended clusters of banana plants. Some dwellings were round with grass roofs, while others were constructed of more modern cement bricks, and topped by metal roofs.

At Loitokitok, a wide spot in the road, the bus turned uphill. My first glimpse of the school was of sturdy buildings and tidy grounds with pleasant flowerbeds. I learned that before independence, it had served as a resort for the East African settlers. When the British left, it was commandeered by the new Kenyan government.

I was the first of the temporary female instructors to arrive. We were recruited to fill in for the regular male instructors, most of whom were attending a sea course at the coast. I believed it was designed to get the men out of camp. Mixing men of authority with compliant secondary school girls could be a problem. With women in direct contact with the budding female leaders, the students would be free to fully participate without harassment.

As I approached the dining hall for lunch, a small, trim African with a neat mustache approached me. His well-pressed khaki clothing and his excellent posture suggested he was a military man. John introduced himself as the camp director, welcomed me without a smile and told me to meet him after lunch. As he strode away, his abrupt, no-nonsense manner made me wonder how much guidance I would receive for my temporary role as an instructor. This was my first exposure to leadership training. While I had been a summer camp counselor and a student advisor in college, I had never been trained to lead. I had a lot to learn.

John found me after our meal and, without explanation, told me to follow him. Not far from the buildings we entered a grove of tall evergreens with a giant playground: logs, old tires, ropes, cables, and nets strung in the shade. *What fun!* I thought.

"This is our ropes course," John said. "We use this to build confidence in the students. Each challenge is designed to look difficult, but they are easier than they seem and eventually most of the participants succeed. You will be demonstrating this tomorrow morning. I will explain how they all work and leave you to try them out."

"O.K.," I said, suddenly alert.

I studied the rope bridges and ladders, balance beams, Tarzan-like swings, high pulley slides, and slack balance ropes. Several shallow pools of water lay underneath, just deep enough to add an element of humiliation to falling.

"You will not be able to practice the zip line today because I have to show you how to put on the safety gear and I don't have the time for that right now," John said.

He pointed up. About thirty feet in the air a skinny horizontal pole was tied between two trees; a thin cord drooped about four feet above it. A few feet higher, a taut cable ran between the trunks. From the right-hand tree, another cable sloped down to pass through a thick cargo net suspended at the bottom. The zip line looked terrific, if a person could manage to traverse the pole to grab the pulley handle and leap into space to slide down into the net.

John left. So I practiced. In a half hour, I finished what I could of the course. My only problem was with a balance log resembling a giant teeter-totter. When I gingerly stepped onto it and up the steep side to the mid-point, the log began to sway. It wasn't like a small plank on a playground; the heavy weight changed the dynamics. At the balance point, I slowed and gradually shifted my weight, struggling to swing the log gracefully to the other side. I feared the sudden impact would throw me off into a pool of water. I made it but was irritated because falling off such a simple challenge would be disgraceful.

Back at the main campus, I found Neila Helmholtz, my friend and fellow Peace Corps volunteer. She was chatting with George Brose, also in our PCV group. George had recently joined the permanent OBMS staff. I looked forward to spending a little time with them both, since I hadn't seen them for several months.

Neila and I settled into our small room with twin beds and a bathroom and then joined the other temps for our meeting with John. We were all white teachers from East African secondary schools. John arrived and wasted no time telling us that he would instruct us on what to do and we would then tell the students. When we split up for expeditions, he would lead half the camp and George would follow a day or two later with the other half. John instructed us on the evening's task and then dismissed. As I left, I was filled with excitement and anticipation.

After dinner, we met the students. There were about eighty girls altogether from secondary schools in Kenya, Tanzania, and Uganda. About eight were white, twenty were Asians, and the rest were Africans. Each patrol had a mix of races. I introduced myself to my patrol and after brief introductions, gave them their first challenge: they were to name their group. My job was to observe which students were talking, who stayed silent, and who influenced others. After a spirited discussion, they named themselves *"Faru,"* which means rhinoceros. I was busy trying to remember their names and neglected to take any notes on their interactions, something I regretted when I had to evaluate them at the end of the course.

After all the naming was completed, John gave a clipped and emotionless overview of the next three weeks. Teamwork was paramount, he stressed, and leadership a close second. The needs of the patrol members would come before the leaders' needs. Each day, the patrols were to choose among themselves a different captain and quartermaster so that each student would experience both positions of responsibility.

I was disappointed that John seemed so distant. Maybe it was his military background, or maybe he wasn't used to dealing with women. "Do this." The end. Where was that enthusiastic leader who could whip the group into an eager frenzy for action? George said later that the chief instructor for the school was at the coast, which may have explained John's lack of enthusiasm.

At 6:30 a.m., a scratchy recording of a bugle-playing reveille filled the camp. Neila and I, dressed in swimsuits and tennies, stood in the chilly air, teeth chattering. We rubbed our goose-pimply arms in a vain attempt to get warm as the instructors and students gathered. At last, but not soon enough for me, we sped into the forest for our first run. Just as that lovely warm feeling allowed me to relax, we broke into a clearing and stood on the lip of an old swimming pool. The site was surrounded by a dense stand of trees. I doubted much sun ever reached it. Cold, fresh water from the slopes of Kilimanjaro gushed out of a pipe at the end of the pool. John stood at the other end, fully dressed and shouted, "Jump in!" urging us to swim to the other side. The only exception was for students who could not swim.

I sucked in the morning air and jumped. A tumult of gasps and splashing assaulted me as I surfaced. My own voice was loud in my ears. We swam for speed, not grace, and vaulted out the other side. Our shoes dripped and squished as we raced back to our rooms.

The students had to do the run every day. We temps took turns being Duty Instructor. That person is the only instructor who has to do the morning run with the girls. Toweling off after my warm shower, I calculated that I'd have to lead at least two morning runs. Mind over matter and all. These British and their stiff upper lips! Grumbling through aching teeth, I uttered every stereotype and cliché I could recall that would fit the situation and some that wouldn't. Neila stepped out of the shower and overheard my monologue. She lightly offered to do my morning run duty because she enjoyed it.

"Alright!" I said. Whatever she wanted in return was worth it.

After breakfast, while the students tidied up the camp, we instructors had another meeting with John. He let us know he would only be interacting with the students when his expertise was needed. He would meet with us periodically to give us instructions. I was thankful, because that was enough contact for me. I was beginning to dislike the man.

After a military-style inspection, we gathered on the open lawn, the mountain and evergreen forest on one side and the plains below us to the north. In the increasing heat, John read quotes from famous leaders, followed by announcements. His delivery was flat. He briefed us on the schedule for the day, where each patrol would be during the eight-course periods. Half the camp, including my patrol, was assigned to the ropes course for the morning.

That would be me, demonstrating, I realized.

John led the four patrols into the grove of trees and the welcomed shade. I caught a glimpse of the white peak and gasped. Kilimanjaro! There it stood.

But first we had to prepare.

"This is our ropes course. It is your first challenge. By the end of the course, you all should be able to successfully complete this circuit. Remember that your patrol comes first, so encourage your patrol members as they meet the challenges."

He turned to me.

"Miss Denison will demonstrate how it is done."

Fueled by adrenaline and in denial that anything could go wrong, I made it through the balance beam, the teeter-totter log, and a few other obstacles with pools of water glinting below.

Then I stood at the base of the thick tree trunk and looked up at the zip line, wondering how it was done. The forty students gathered around.

John grabbed a six-foot piece of rope and held up a metal oval with a snap link. "This is a carabiner," he said. "You'll use these in the ropes course and later when we get to the rocks."

He showed me how to secure the rope around my waist. With the rope end in my hand, carabiner dangling down, I stood ready. Facing the eager young women, John said, "Now, this is your safety. As you move through this challenge, this carabiner," he grabbed the metal oval, "must always be connected to a safety cable so if you fall, it will only be a short distance."

Falling a short distance wouldn't be bad, I thought, *but hanging by just a rope around my waist would certainly smart.*

He signaled me to climb up a makeshift ladder: two metal cables spliced with narrow wooden steps, fastened tightly to the tree. I reached up as high as I could to snap the safety carabiner on to the cable, climbed above that point, and reclipped it higher up. It seemed simple, except the steps abutted the tree so I had trouble working my foot in far enough to feel really secure. I could only put my weight on my toes, which did not make me feel at all secure. Maybe the steps were deliberately fashioned as such. They looked simple, felt hard, but were really easy, as John had said.

I clutched each rung and went up, not too distressed because I had climbed trees as a kid, though not usually with an audience. When my feet reached the horizontal pole at the top, John called up to hold tight and move the "biner" to the high cable stretched between the trees. Done. I hugged the grooved bark and managed to step around the trunk and onto the pole, my back to the tree.

He shouted up from below: the cable was only for safety, not for my use, but I could hang on to the little bitty string that hung loosely at shoulder height. With my back securely against that wonderfully solid trunk, I grabbed the string and realized its help was only psychological. I looked down into forty pairs of trusting eyes. Adrenaline rushed through my veins. I sucked in a deep breath, stepped out, and somehow had that other tree in my arms in a flash. What luck! I was almost done.

The next part looked easy.

Foolish me.

I was to sidle around that tree, stand on the pole that extended another four feet past the trunk, reach up and back, and unsnap the "biner." I was to snap it on to the zip line, the cable above me that plunged to the ground at a 30-degree angle. It was a slide, after all, not a free fall. A cord attached to my tree was attached to a pulley with a handle, located at the bottom of the zip line. My back to the tree, I pulled the cord to bring up the pulley. It stopped just out of my reach. Three inches more! The handle dangled, teasing me. All I had to do was to let go of the tree, grab the handle, and zip off.

I needed more hands. One, preferably two hands for the tree, plus one hand for the handle, and another hand to hold the cord lest the pulley zip back down without me.

So, I understood what I was supposed to do. Tree. Handle. Zip. The problem was I couldn't grab the pulley handle and hold on to the tree at the same time. They were just a little too far apart. What a diabolical design. I had to let go, take a step and grab. All those eyes watching. Actually, I'd forgotten about the eyes. My attention was on remembering to breathe and reminding myself that this was designed to look difficult, but was really easy.

After what seemed like a millennium, I stepped free of the tree, grabbed the pulley handle with both hands, and wow! Wind in my face and a thrill in my belly. I remembered to tuck my knees up to the side, as instructed, to prevent rupturing my spleen when I struck the net. I hit it in good form. The ride was way too short, but I didn't ask for a rerun.

The students coached and cheered each other through the course with great enthusiasm, the most cheering for the ones who had trouble. I proudly thought my patrol would do well as a team.

On the second day, they stepped up and down, on and off chairs for a cardio test. I took their pulses at intervals and helped with the record keeping. Chris Field, the nurse, who also taught the first aid course and feminine hygiene, ran the tests. The girls got some protocol on personal cleanliness, how to poop in the bush, and how to take care of menstrual issues for those not accustomed to living outside. I was glad they were paying attention to bathroom issues since the school used the same routes for all its expeditions. I wasn't eager to find left-behinds from other groups.

In the days that followed, John briefed us temps twice a day in his disengaged monotone. Maybe he needed a new job. We passed the instructions on to the students. They strengthened their bodies with runs, volleyball games, and fitness exercises at 6,000 feet. They took classes on knot tying, map reading, first aid, rescue procedures, and leadership skills. The non-swimmers got a short course in drown-proofing. About the time we fell into a daily rhythm, it all changed....

Harriet

MONDAY, AUGUST 10, 1967

Dear Everyone,

At the morning meeting of instructors, John announced our first expedition. After he told the students, the room buzzed with excitement. Being active at the higher altitude of the school had given most of them confidence to deal with the climb.

John laid out the next few days. He would lead the four patrols and instructors in my half of the camp part way up Mt. Kilimanjaro. The students would do a solo overnight, some rock climbing, spend another night, and return to camp. The other half would follow in our steps two days later with George leading.

That afternoon we organized equipment and food. The students divided up group items like cooking pots,

rice, and oatmeal, so each wound up with a load pro-
portional to her weight. Picture a dizzying array of old
British Army equipment: boots, jackets, packs, gloves,
sleeping bags, ponchos, canteens, and pots. The lawn
resembled a giant rummage sale as the girls tried
on items they needed until they found ones that fit.
I had my own boots and sleeping bag so I helped the
students, snagging the remaining equipment I needed.

In the morning, I hoisted my 30-pound pack and
waved goodbye to Neila, George, and the students
who remained behind. As they returned to their
training, our line of students and instructors spread
along the trail that wound through grasses and shrub
toward the forest. John was last to leave, but quickly
overtook the line.

Still early in the day, the first leg was not too hot,
but I was glad to reach the shade of the trees. Lichen
dripped from the fat limbs. Ferns dotted the thick
ground moss, reminding me of Oregon. Among the
familiar evergreens were some odd looking 30-foot
tree ferns. Moss draped the skinny trunks, their tops
crowned with a spray of filigreed fronds, not something
you would find in Oregon.

Most of the girls walked quietly, delightful after the
frenzied preparations. I remained at the back of the
line with one of the other instructors making sure no
one was left behind. Our reverie was broken when one
of the students dropped back and told us she was just
not able to keep up. I reminded her that she should
be telling her patrol and letting them help her. She
stayed with us until we encountered the others up
the trail. The leaders of the day had done the right
thing when they realized she was not with them. They
stopped to see if she might appear and while waiting,
they discussed a Plan B. That was a good sign that the
team was gelling.

They set off at a somewhat slower pace and a few of her patrol fell back to encourage her.

Soon, we were out of the forest and onto the moorlands. We picked our way up among the exposed rock, isolated clumps of grass, and the fat-leaved succulents able to survive above tree line.

By a little stream we dropped our packs and dug into them for our basic, no-frills lunches. I had never eaten sardines out of a tin, but after the vigorous hike, the first tiny fish was the finest snack I had ever tasted. A sleeve of dry soda crackers filled in the holes and sopped up the olive oil. After the sardines were gone, I poured oil from the tin straight into my mouth. Even that tasted delicious. A carrot, a piece of fruit, and a candy bar for dessert. Sated and tired, I lay back on the grass in the warm sun. Just as my eyes were closing for a lovely nap, John called out, "Time to go!"

Around three, we stopped for the day. My patrol was last to arrive and we gratefully shrugged off our packs. The rest of the students were scattered among the short, gray-green succulents. Exhaustion muted conversation among the tired girls. I sat briefly and stared at rosettes of yellow daisy-like flowers on long stems. I could pull petals or make daisy chains. My brain was too tired to decide.

Too soon, John gathered us together. Firmly in command, hands on his hips, he laid out the next event.

"Your challenge now is to set up a solo camp for yourself. You will be placed in a spot that is isolated from the other girls." Some of the students glanced around, looking a bit uneasy.

"The first thing you will do is to build a bivouac, a lean-to shelter for protection in case of rain. You must start a fire for warmth and to cook your meals. You will need some warm food in your bellies. It will be cold tonight. You are not to contact anyone else or come back to this camp unless you have a serious emergency. Your patrol leader will check on you twice before you go to sleep to make certain you are adequately prepared for the night."

John gave each instructor a box of wooden matches. I handed out four matches to each student in *Faru* patrol. The weary girls stood up, helped each other put on their packs, and followed me. I placed them close to the path, far enough apart so they could not see or hear each other but close enough that I could find them without trouble.

An hour later, most were doing fine. The available material was easy to work with, bushes with brittle limbs that could be tied in bundles and lashed onto a simple lean-to frame. Some of the students had stretched the school-issued poncho over the frame, which was allowed. Even I could have passed the bivouac test, after seeing how they managed, but I might have been stumped if I had just been plopped on my solo site as they had. Most of them were feeding bits of fuel to small but lively fires. The African girls just got to work, ate, and were soon in bed. The white European student was coping, but two of the Asians were having a lot of trouble. Their bivouacs were shaky; they had no fire, and looked very sad. I made a few suggestions and left them at their work.

The instructors' bivouac was a musty, semi-permanent structure of the same material one-degree sturdier than what the girls were building. It was just large enough for the four of us. John, the only man, took the small cozy annex, for which I was glad.

In conversation with the other instructors, we found the same general abilities prevailed among the three ethnic groups. We speculated that the Africans had experience building with available materials, even if they lived in cities now. Most of the European students were children of settlers. Some had grown up on farms, often living close to the African staff and free to wander the bush if they were so inclined. However, the Asian families who lived in East Africa were storekeepers. Traditionally, they kept a close rein on their girls and women, letting hired Africans do the menial work. The shelter building seemed unfamiliar to the Asian girls and sleeping alone for the first time was a major challenge for them. The girls were selected for their leadership potential, not necessarily for other skills.

Two of the instructors, who were physical education majors, mentioned that they were using birth control pills to regulate their periods. They often continued taking them past the normal number of days to prevent the onset when a big event was approaching. I had never taken the pill and was stunned that it could be used in such a way. To have such control over a pesky monthly occurrence was an eye opener.

At dusk on my second circuit, I made certain everyone had a fire going. The sun was down and it was getting chilly. Neither of the struggling Asian girls had a fire, so I pulled out my box of kitchen matches. Luckily, I had lots. I never had built a campfire using those materials myself, and it took me way too many matches to accomplish the task. Embarrassing, indeed.

Tired after my last check of the girls, I fell asleep quickly and stayed toasty in spite of the mountain chill. On the morning round, all the students had eaten and were packing up. A few confessed their night was not overly restful, but all were cheerful and ready for the day. I ate quickly and we were off, hiking up to the next camp.

At about 11,000 feet, about 1 p.m., we dropped our packs near volcanic formations in the side of the mountain. We gazed into caves formed from huge flat bubbles of gases that had solidified before bursting at the surface. In time, one side of the cave had eroded to open the space.

In the two caves where we stopped, rock piles at the edges showed attempts by previous visitors to create comfortable sleeping spots. The larger cave was big enough to hold two patrols overnight. The third patrol took a smaller cave nearby. John assigned my patrol to a cave a short walk down a side trail, past several smaller but unusable caves. Finding a spot without rocks for the night would be a challenge in our assigned cave, but we had no time for that. Our instructions were to drop our packs, eat lunch, and return with our water and an extra layer of clothing. He didn't say anything about a flashlight or poncho, which I discovered later, would have been useful. All we knew was that we would be rock climbing that afternoon, something new for all of us. We ate quickly and joined the others.

From the caves, John led us upward for half an hour until we stopped at the base of a wide rock wall perhaps 100 feet high. Four ropes hung from the top. The sharp dark rocks reminded me of the basalt of Mt. Hood, near my Oregon home, where the enormous hexagonal columns threw enchanting shadows in the right light.

We settled in amidst the scrub brush to hear what would come next. John planted his feet with his back to the wall, waiting for quiet. A few girls moved in from the edges so they could hear.

"The object of the exercise is for every member of the patrol to climb to the top of the cliff. Each patrol will use one of the ropes hanging behind me. It will be attached to the climber at the waist, supplemented by a figure eight loop around the thighs. It is only for safety. You will not use it while you climb. One of your team will sit at the top, tie herself to a rock, and manage the upper end of the safety rope, slowly pulling it in so if the climber falls, she will catch her and the climber will not be injured. The person on the top is the belayer. When you get to the top, you will become the belayer and the person you replace will walk down an easier route to the bottom."

He demonstrated how the belayer should tie herself securely to a rock. Then, she was to wrap the rope from the climber around her waist and brace herself.

John added, "When the belayer is set, she calls out 'On belay.'

"If you are the climber, once tied into the harness and ready to climb, you yell out, to your belayer, 'Climbing.' She will respond with, 'Climb on.'

"Climbing is not difficult. Use both hands and both feet. There are lots of handholds and steps, just feel around. As you get higher off the ground, look up and not down. The one thing to remember for safety is to anchor your hands and feet well. Move only one at a time. Remember that you'll make it to the top by yourself. The rope is only for safety.

"To demonstrate for yourself this is safe, when you are about ten feet up, call out to your belayer 'falling.' At that point, you are to jump away from the cliff. You will see that the belayer really will hold you in a fall. Then you can continue. Belayers, you must assume that the climber could fall at any moment, so be prepared."

The first belayers followed John up a trail on one side of the climbing wall and settled into their positions. I joined the Faru Patrol at the bottom of our rope to cheer on our climbers.

Miriam, our most confident team member, stepped forward and grabbed the dangling rope. She tied on, called up, got the go-ahead and started climbing. When she called out, "Falling," she shrieked in surprise when she dropped, but only fell a few feet before the rope caught her. From there, she did quite well, finding good hand and footholds for her climb. We called up holds we could see from below and she continued easily to the top.

Some girls walked up as if the cliff were a staircase. Others needed encouragement, which the patrol was ready to give. One by one, the students climbed the face, discovering it was not that difficult. John patrolled the rim, checking the belayers.

Gradually, fog blew in and obscured the sunlight. We pulled out our extra layers, but I could see the students looking around for shelter from the light wind. Only a few bushes were thick enough to help. Some girls began to shiver.

Most students had finished climbing when John came down off the cliff to see how many had not done the climb. I pointed out that it was beginning to get dark and the girls were getting cold. Perhaps the climbing had taken longer than expected. I couldn't imagine making them climb in the dark. I wondered out loud if we should stop.

John said, "No. Every student has to make it to the top." As a junior instructor, I bit my lip. I didn't like the risk of staying too long on the exposed rocks, half an hour from warm food, our gear, and our cozy cave. He must have a plan.

The next *Faru* Patrol member was moving well about half way up the cliff when her foot slipped. She screamed and fell, unable to warn her belayer. This was not the planned fall. Though she was not seriously hurt, she was banged and shaken enough for concern.

"I'm sending *Faru* Patrol back," John said abruptly.

Was it just to get rid of me? I wondered. He gave me directions to our cave by way of a shortcut. "Just follow the path back and take the first left." It sounded so easy.

The light was dim as we started out, and soon we were unable to see the path. Two girls found tiny keychain flashlights in their pockets. We put one in front and one in the middle, held hands, and groped our way toward our cave. Fortunately, the path was deeply worn and lined with thick grasses. At the intersection John had told me to look for, the tiny flashlights were dimming. The fog had obscured what starlight might have helped. The side path we were to take was not well defined. The situation felt dangerous. I was afraid I might not only get lost myself, but also take the whole patrol with me. I conferred with the patrol members. They agreed we should wait for John.

When John arrived with the other three patrols, it was pitch black. He was familiar with the trail but was angry we had waited. "The side path would take you right to the cave," he said. He urged us to go that direction.

By that point, I knew that his style of directions and time estimates didn't match mine. I feared we could walk right by the cave without knowing it.

"No," I said.

No one else had a light that might help us. We followed John, stumbling in the dark, everyone holding hands for balance.

At the large cave we managed to borrow a few flashlights and set out for our cave. It was 10 p.m. Maybe in the dark the distances are deceiving, but as we struggled on I began to think we were going to have to spend the night in the open. The first cave we encountered was too rocky for an impromptu bivouac. The next one was worse. I didn't relish the idea of just stopping to wait for daylight. We had none of our equipment—no food, sleeping bags, or tarps, so we pressed on.

Even with the flashlights, we were lost. We conferred as a group and pressed on. Somehow we found our cave at 11 p.m. We all fell into our sleeping bags, exhausted. No one was interested in the hassle of a fire even with the promise of hot food.

I was angry with John for his irresponsible leadership. Looking back, I knew we should have taken flashlights and more layers with us that afternoon. He should have known about the shifts in weather and light near the climbing wall. Should the safety of the group come second in importance to everyone doing the climb? How could climbing in the dark be safe? Perhaps he'd misjudged my ability to lead the patrol when he sent us back early, or perhaps it was my own personal challenge. If so, I hadn't met it particularly well, which made me feel worse.

The next morning the fears of the night had faded, the challenges seemed less daunting. After a filling breakfast of oatmeal thickly dotted with raisins, we turned downhill.

By 1:30 p.m., we reached the home camp. Ugly blisters had formed on my heels. My little toes were very sore. I vowed to pay more attention to my feet next time I left camp and to be careful when dealing with John.

Harriet

FRIDAY, AUGUST 14, 1967

Dear Family,

After more physical conditioning and orienteering classes, and practicing with maps and compasses, it was time to test the students' abilities. Our next challenge was in the bush: a flat landscape flanked by the Tsavo and Amboseli Game Reserves.

Recently, one of the school employees had speared a lion near the school grounds after three lions killed one of his cows. Cape Buffalo were not uncommon. Elephants roamed the slopes of Kilimanjaro. To check for problem animals and see the region, a few of us temps climbed into the Land Rover and drove north out of camp, on to the plains.

The dry grasses, prickly bushes, and flat-topped acacia trees were home to hundreds of predators and thousands of ungulates, such as gazelles and impalas. Usually, we followed a visible track, but occasionally darted off to check out a suspicious lion-sized bush. Lions will occupy hunting territories and defend them from other lions, but we found none. Nor did we see other dangerous animals like Cape Buffalo, elephants, or rhinos. John had assured us that the ungulates we did see would not be a problem, so we returned, confident our students would be safe.

Each patrol would walk a different zigzag route, competing to see which patrol could best finish the assigned tasks. To avoid our influence, each of the instructors would monitor a patrol not their own. On the morning my half of the camp departed, I had my last meeting with *Faru* Patrol and wished them good luck.

I climbed into the transport truck and joined a new patrol. We rumbled and bumped down the dusty road, squinting into the breeze of our motion. When we stopped half an hour later, the breeze died as well. The warm mid-morning hinted at the heat to come. Dropping to the ground, we grabbed our daypacks and checked our water.

John gave the patrol the clue to their first control point and drove off. Under the shade of one of the few trees, the students laid out their maps. I stood back. They read the clue, marked the map, calculated the compass reading, set their compasses, and marched off into the bush.

I trailed behind them, picking my way carefully past dry brush with three-inch thorns, thickets of bushes, and clumps of trees. Though we saw no dangerous animals, we watched in awe the herds of striped zebras and slender-necked, honey-colored gazelles, and their relatives. A few grunting wildebeests grazed their way past us. A large male was usually on watch for each herd. Sometimes, the nearest animals would take a step or two away from us, but casually, as if they were going to do that anyway. Near a herd of zebras, we infringed on their comfort zone. The male snorted a warning. The nearest ones jerked their heads, trotted off a short way and resumed grazing.

The students did a great job. At each control point they had to look for a tree, a rock, or a hole in the ground to find a can with the next set of directions. The bush was very flat with few physical points of reference except, of course, Mount Kilimanjaro to the southwest. They had to be fairly accurate with their compass directions or they would spend fruitless time looking under the wrong tree or rock. Since so few trees and rocks were in the area, the exercise proved easier than I had anticipated. Only later did I discover it was not so easy for other patrols.

I enjoyed a lovely walk among the animals and birds, happily tagging along behind the able students, wondering when I might be needed.

They stopped. With the map central to their deliberations, they pointed ahead to something and then back to the map. More pointing and animated discussion. Finally, a girl walked back to where I waited.

"Please, madam. May I ask a question?" she said respectfully.

I nodded.

"We have calculated the direction we need to go but there is a problem. If we follow our compass course, we will be walking through a family of giraffes that are grazing on the trees ahead. We will do that if you tell us it is our only choice, but we are certain that if we go around them, we will be able to resume the line on the other side of the trees."

I walked forward until I could see the giraffe family. They stood, noses high, in a thicket of acacias, agile lips grasping the leafy branchlets and munching quietly—all except the large male who watched us closely. The baby, too short for the trees, weaved its way through the legs of the adults, returning to Mama for a suck. I thought the giraffes would just move if the students approached, but since the baby might influence their reaction, I told the girls to go around.

At last, I felt useful.

I walked from the shade of one tree to another. Heat radiated off the sunbaked dirt but the temperature, in the 80s °F, was not unpleasant. It was the warm end of the rainy season. Termites fascinate me, so I detoured to peek down a tall mound. The lateritic clay of the plains dries so hard the local people use it on the floors of their huts. It polishes smooth as tile. Peering inside the mound, I was disappointed that I couldn't see past the first few feet in the dark. My flashlight was in my overnight pack at the camp. No termites were on the outside of the mound—no surprise because, in my lab, they always built mud tunnels to get from one place to another, avoiding the desiccating sun.

I felt safe in the dry grass that was over my head at times, but not thick enough to hide a large animal. Night would be different when the predators hunted.

My new patrol was the first and only one to reach Camp One before the 3:30 p.m. deadline. We had been told there would be extra water and a snack for us, but all we found was a heap of rolled canvas tents with a note from John saying not to put them up until he arrived. Thirst made me cranky. I would have loved a Wright's biscuit or two, but the students took it in stride. We each found a spot of shade, made ourselves comfortable, chatted, or napped. Another patrol arrived an hour later. By the time John showed up at 5:45 p.m., all four patrols were waiting.

The tardy patrols lost marks. *Faru* Patrol dragged in last of all. John had stressed that we were not leaders for our patrols, but were only there to convey information. Still, I felt close to the *Faru* girls and was a little disappointed they had arrived last. I should have been happy they actually found the camp that day.

Three instructors who had been unable to hike, climbed out of John's Land Rover. I was annoyed and a little sanctimonious that they hadn't been out in the bush with the rest of us. Neila was still in camp with the other patrols, so I didn't even have her to share my complaints. Silently I called them shirkers, lollygaggers. I even made up a few names, but I knew I was just generally crabby. John irritated me as well, not leaving the water and snack he had promised with the pile of tents. We could have used the afternoon to set up camp. I resented the wasted time.

We instructors unrolled our tent while the girls worked on theirs. By the time we were pounding stakes, the daylight was almost gone.

The next day, the other half of the school was to follow in our footsteps. That was the plan, but in the bush, chaos reigned.

In the morning, my half gathered around John. He stood at the bottom of the tallest tree to give us a demonstration of how to rig up for abseiling, known in the U.S. as repelling, the descent of rock climbing.

Here's how it went: at the top of a cliff and using the now familiar harness, you tie yourself to a rope secured to a rock or tree. The belayer holds the safety line. You wrap a second rope between your legs, up your back, and over your shoulder. Your patrol mate pays out the safety line—as opposed to reeling it in on belay. When ready, you turn away from the edge and take one thrilling step backwards into space to start sliding down the rope.

How do you control the descent? You let out the rope with your hand. Pull back to create more friction and slow the descent, or forward to drop faster. If you're comfortable with plunging earthward on a skinny string, you can take giant strides down the cliff face, but the heat from the friction will slow the most daring.

I was unable to watch the abseilers and took the truck back to the main camp. My period had started unexpectedly, probably due to our time at the higher altitude. I hoped that had accounted for my frustration the previous night. For a few hours I did laundry, gathered supplies, and waited for a vehicle. Finally, I got word that a truck was departing soon for Camp One with a few other people.

The camp was deserted when we arrived, so we helped unload the truck. The equipment was for the second four patrols that would arrive in the afternoon. No snacks awaited them, either. The driver had to go back to the school and he told us John would come by to pick us up and take us to Camp Two.

Two hours later, John appeared. I was hot, thirsty, and steaming. He had been searching for two patrols from the first group that had not found the abseiling rock and were not at Camp Two, either. We waited to see if they might show up where we were at Camp One. By 5:30, most of them dragged in. One patrol had lost three of their members. Two patrols in the second half of the school had arrived as well, but the other two were still in the bush.

We called, whistled, and yelled for the missing students without response. A number of us still had to get to Camp Two for the night. John only had the Land Rover. It was too small to move the girls and staff and the gear he needed to move as well. We piled the gear and our packs in the vehicle. I walked the students in the direction of the second camp, which was not too far away as the crow flies. John unloaded, then shuttled us to Camp Two and left again to search for the missing students.

In the morning, we learned that the last two patrols of the second half finally did show up at Camp One, but in spite of calls, whistles, and searches, three missing students spent the night in the bush. They were actually not far from that camp, which they found the next morning. Luckily, no lions, elephants, rhinos, or hyenas found them.

I wondered why John was not more concerned. Perhaps our scouting of the area had assured him that the girls were safe. Perhaps, had they not found the camp on their own, we might have been mustered to rescue them. As it was, my half of the camp set off for the school after breakfast while we instructors waited for a lift, which arrived later in the day.

All in all, I was enjoying the Outward Bound experience but was disappointed with John's leadership. I hoped the rest of the course would not be such a struggle for me and that I wouldn't be ejected for my own incompetence.

Harriet

SUNDAY, AUGUST 20, 1967

Dear All,

Mount Kilimanjaro waited while classes and physical conditioning resumed. Each person prepared for the final expedition with excitement, some with a touch of fear. I'd only hiked a few lesser peaks in central Oregon on trips that took a day up and back. Kilimanjaro rose to 19,000 feet. Its legends were many; for one, Hemingway's frozen leopard described in his book, *The Snows of Kilimanjaro*. Really, Kilimanjaro isn't much more than a big volcanic hill that pokes out of the plains of East Africa, but if you've never done any climbing, the unknown looms large.

Finally, John announced it was time. Once again, we checked our equipment, added warm sweaters, jackets, pants, and balaclavas, and most important, the school's dark goggles. The air is so thin at high altitudes that special snow goggles were crucial to protect our eyes from the equatorial sun. Each patrol was issued a few tubes of zinc oxide to totally block the sun's rays from delicate noses and lips. Even the dark skin of the African girls could burn.

Eight porters were hired to give us a little help with our loads. Each of us was allowed to weigh and label one pound of our allotted group food for the men to carry to the school's hut near the peak. Once again, we shifted group equipment to divide weight among our packs. My pack weighed about thirty-five pounds.

On the big day, the students skipped the run but ate a hearty breakfast and tidied up. In excited clusters, they assembled at the trailhead. Sick and injured girls who were staying behind gathered to wish their comrades good luck. Hugs all around were followed by the commotion of hoisting packs. Everyone had an assistant to help with the final adjustments. With a vigorous wave from the girls staying behind, the students turned their backs on the camp and began the climb.

The patrols had coalesced well. We knew the students would look out for each other on the trail they had hiked previously, so the instructors and John had the privilege of riding a little way up the mountain to the edge of the forest, which put us about 45 minutes closer to our destination. Neila and I set out at the end of the line of students at about 10:30 a.m. We had passed all but two patrols by about 4:30 p.m., when we arrived at the second caves. *Faru* Patrol was settling into our familiar cave. Most of us relaxed in the sun while student cooks prepared a splendid hot meal. After eating, we climbed into our bags for a good night's rest.

On the second day, a few more girls dropped out. Some were too tired to continue and some suffered from altitude sickness that brings on headaches and labored breathing. That small group stayed at the caves to wait our return. Neila and I started behind the students again at 8:45 a.m. About an hour above the caves, we filled our water containers for the last time from the stream we had been following. It was cool and delicious. I felt anxious about leaving the water source as the path turned upslope.

We tramped over rises and into valleys, always up and up. In one canyon, we found giant *senecios,* or groundsels, unique to the slopes of Kilimanjaro. Their fat, shaggy trunks grew as tall as fir trees. The only visible growing part was at the top. Floppy green rosettes of arrow-shaped leathery leaves looked tiny on the thick trunks. The trees' shaggy layers of drooping dead leaves protected them from the sun and cold.

We just walked up and up and up on the trail that wound through a new array of desert plants, dry grasses, and gray-green ground covers with crisp papery flowers. When the vegetation all but ended, we crunched between large lava rocks perched on the grit.

The bright glare of sun warmed where it hit me, but my shaded side was cool. Walking evened out our body warmth and we were able to shed a few layers. The rest stops were short so we wouldn't get chilled. We caught our breath the best we could in the rarified air and moved on.

Our target for that day was the Outward Bound School hut at 15,000 feet. Over a small rise, I finally made out some straight lines on the horizon that I recognized, with relief, to be a hut. Approaching us were the porters of our precious food, on their return trip. The eight of them passed with a slight nod. At about 1 o'clock I arrived, the first woman to reach the hut, though the others were not far behind. John, George, and another male instructor stood near the door. Next to them were the packs of food, along with extra fuel and water for cooking.

The rugged, well-weathered wooden structure looked too small for the number of people arriving shortly. We were down to sixty-one students and seven staff, including the three men from the regular staff and four women instructors. The men told us to have the girls drop their packs outside in piles by patrol and stay there. While the latecomers straggled in, the early arrivals found relatively rock-free spots of grit and stretched out for a little snooze.

The sun descended rapidly. A finger of fog crept over the ridge above us. The wind cooled the hikers. By late afternoon, they had to keep moving to stay warm, walking slowly or jiggling in place. The last students to straggle in were at an advantage because they had less time to sit and get cold. When everyone had arrived, each patrol leader was told to collect the sleeping bags and put them on the hut floor by patrol.

With no fuel available at that altitude, the men cooked for everyone on Primus stoves, part of the hut's equipment. We female instructors unrolled the sleeping bags and spread them flat, overlapping so they all would fit in the tiny space.

Dinner was a thick soup, coffee, and a few crackers that we served to the students as they waited outside. While we cleaned up, they brushed their teeth and reorganized their packs for the next day. It was an early and a short night. The girls entered by patrols and found their sleeping bags. When they snaked themselves into the bags they discovered they were so close they all had to sleep on the same side. In the night, they all turned together with grace and grumbling. However, they were warm as toasty sardines. We instructors had a bit more room. We didn't have to spoon, but I did get a little chilly.

At 2 a.m., the cooks awoke to prepare the breakfast oatmeal. The students were not allowed to get up yet in the frigid hut, which was fine with them. We passed out bowls of hot cereal for them to eat in their bags to retain as much heat as possible.

Then, in a flurry of activity, we all jumped into our warmest clothing to begin the final push to the top. I had worn my tennies hiking up to the hut because I got blisters on our first hike up the mountain. The blisters had healed well enough for me to put on my heavy socks and boots for that final climbing day. The boots were warmer and more stable on the rocks.

A few more students chose to remain at the hut, nursing headaches and sore feet. They were left to clean up the breakfast dishes. At 4 a.m., forty-seven students and all the instructors gathered outside in silence, eager to begin, our sleep-warmth seeping out of us in the chilly predawn.

Neila and I were assigned our places in the line. We wished each other luck and began walking. Bright starlight illuminated the rocks as John led us up the stark mountainside. The crunch of our boots on the gritty lava got louder as we settled into line behind him. Maybe it was a good thing that we were not all wide-awake: better just to keep the feet moving. I took my place toward the rear to keep an eye on the students. As we plodded on and got our blood moving, the bitter cold became inconsequential, but the lack of oxygen was more pronounced. I was up to two breaths per step.

After an hour of snaking upwards, a few more students were ready to quit. We planted them on the trail next to a large rock for a little shelter with stern instructions to wait for our return. They would be chilly for a while, but after the sun rose they would be fine.

At 6 a.m., we left more students next to the trail. My head felt fat, the beginning of a headache, but I pushed on with the others. As the sky began to lighten, the sun crept around Mawenzi, the lesser peak on Kilimanjaro to the west. Tourists usually stayed their last night in a hut at the base of Mawenzi, one of three overlapping volcanic cones that make up Mount Kilimanjaro. Then they would trudge across a route up the far side of Kibo, the highest of the three volcanic cones, to meet the same trail we were hiking. On our more northerly route, we climbed directly to Kibo. We had the advantage over most people because we had been living for more than two weeks at six thousand feet and had made the first foray up the slopes already. Still, we gasped for air.

At 7:30 a.m., we reached the bottom of the snowfield that covered a good part of the last slope on Kibo. Many of the girls had never seen snow. Tired as they were, their laughs of delight filled the air. But the glee was short lived. Gilman's Point, our destination on the crater's rim, was in view. We still had a long, steep climb ahead, a thousand vertical feet to go to reach the summit.

We began the arduous zigzagging across the crusted layers of snow. Had we started later in the day, the snow would have been mushy and much more difficult to negotiate. My head throbbed with every step, but I was not yet nauseous, for which I was grateful. With each lift of a leaden leg I wondered if it was the last time it would answer my command. Halfway up, I had to pause with every step. I needed six or eight gasps per step. My heart was doing its best. *Are my lungs taking in any oxygen at all?* I wondered. Everyone silently bore the pain of the exertion. There was no spare energy or air for chatting. We each concentrated on the next step, the next breath.

When the first girls reached the top, I silently cheered. If I could just keep going. My body complained everywhere. My lungs, heart, head, legs—all were telling me to give it up. *Go down.* But there was John, standing above us, as if he had flown up there. Maybe he had. Immersed in my own agonies, I envied his apparent ease.

I made the last hundred feet out of sheer stubbornness. At 10:30 a.m., I reached Gilman's Point at 18,500 feet. Students collapsed in awkward positions, too tired to even straighten their legs. I plopped wearily on a rock and concentrated on breathing. Inhale. Exhale. I willed my heart to slow. My chest heaved, but my lungs seemed unable to suck any oxygen.

John told us to drink water and eat a snack, if we could. I forced a bit of a candy bar past the nausea, too tired to vomit. As Neila approached the summit, the girls called out to her, "Come on, Miss Helmholz, you can do it!" She felt as rotten as I did, but she made it, too.

Having made the climb many times, John did not seem as triumphant as the rest of us. He told us that many climbers walk around the crater rim to Uhuru Peak, the highest point on Kibo. At 19,340 feet, it was the true summit of Kilimanjaro. The rim trail was well trod, but it was too late in the day for us to try for it. No one argued. It would be 45 more agonizing minutes to that peak. Many climbers consider Gilman's Point good enough even though it was not the absolute highest point on the rim. Safety over a quibble, I say!

My throbbing brain was going to break through my skull at any moment. I wanted down. I couldn't even take photographs; the view was so far away. My eyes hurt trying to focus. I asked one of the men to take my picture to remind me that I had actually made it.

I rested for half an hour munching snacks and watching the last stragglers struggle up to join our tired group and flop into exhausted heaps. Eventually, I realized I could climb the last 20 feet to a post that marked Gilman's Point to look down into the crater. Once I'd reached the rim, the turquoise blue glacier inside was a glorious reward for my final effort. From the "real" peak on the far side of the huge white crater, I tracked the snow down into the wind-cleared blue ice. I scanned it just in case Hemingway's leopard was really there, but it was hard to concentrate. The ice was enough. I tried to memorize everything. I knew I would never be back. Except for the headache, it was one of those times I wished would last forever.

In all, 33 girls out of the original 80, along with seven instructors, made it to Gilman's Point. When everyone had arrived, had a snack and water, it was time to retrace our hard won steps. Even the latecomers were ready to start down.

Since the snow had turned wet and soggy, we decided to slide down on our feet, which would decrease the altitude quicker. There was no risk of hitting the rocks on the bottom since mushy snow meant our sliding would be of moderate speed. Everyone loved the boot skiing. Our discomforts were momentarily forgotten as silly grins spread over our faces.

Going down, my headache was not quite as intense because my heart was not straining with exertion. At the bottom of the snowfield, we northerners showed the students the delight of a well-thrown snowball. Screams of good-natured snowball fights filled the air.

The bright sun and lighter color of the trail, now obvious, led us downward. We each walked at the pace we could manage, a long thin line of exhausted women headed home.

We found the first group of students we had left behind. They were bored, glad to see us, and happy to rejoin their patrols. As we rested, I noticed several students talking to one of the Asian girls. Her eyes were closed and tears flowed down her cheeks. "I can't see," she whimpered. She had managed to hike up the snowfield and back without anyone realizing she wasn't wearing her goggles. We had all been so immersed in our own physical challenges that no one had noticed her tears. At that point, all we could do was bandage her eyes and lead her down. George carried her over the roughest spots so she wouldn't trip.

Her misery lasted a few days, but she recovered.

On our return to the hut, most of us still had headaches. I suspect now that we were dehydrated, which added to the pain. There would be no water until we were next to the little stream far below.

The students who stayed in the hut had cleaned it, so we quickly packed what we had left there and stumbled down toward our caves for the night. The relief at heading down was dampened by the wretched pain in my head, so I kept moving. At the stream, I filled my water bottle and drank as much as I could. I arrived at the cave at 5:30 p.m. and still felt rotten, but my feet were doing well. I gulped the thick air. My body tingled with the welcome oxygen.

After a good night's sleep, my headache was almost gone, but just climbing out of my sleeping bag was exhausting. A good breakfast helped revive me. All we had to do that day was return to the school. I laced my boots tight to prevent my toes from jamming as I descended.

Halfway, I took a delicious rest stop in the mossy forest to soak my aching feet in the cool stream. Walking in solitude most of the day soothed my grumbles.

After a glorious shower and luscious nap, I lay on my bed, staring at the ceiling. *I did it, I climbed Kilimanjaro!*

The glow of success spread through me. Soon, a joyful exhilaration joined the pleasant exhaustion of a successful climb. By dinner, I felt pretty smug. The students who had made the summit all seemed to have a permanent smile on their faces. Perhaps I had one as well.

Harriet

THURSDAY, AUGUST 24, 1967

Dear Family,

The day after coming off the mountain, we began another set of challenges—the low ropes initiatives. Summit or not, it was time to test the girls' skills and newly acquired confidence. These ropes, close to the ground, were designed to force the teams to problem solve various scenarios. The obvious solution was usually impossible, leaving a lot of room for creativity. As I observed the students collaborate, I envied them. It looked like a lot of fun but we instructors had work to do. We had to nominate an outstanding student.

First, the students had to work closely on a physical challenge. One exercise, for example, required two students to walk along tight parallel cables. As they progressed, the space between the cables widened. To succeed, they had to figure out how to support each other to the end.

In the trust fall, a team member stood on a platform four feet off the ground and turned her back to the edge. Her patrol waited below, ready to catch her. For many, just letting go and starting to tip backwards was terrifying, like the first exciting step repelling down a rock face. In this challenge, they had to trust the team members to catch them.

These exercises led to challenges that involved the entire team. The one I especially liked was The Wall. Quite simply, everyone needed to scale a 10-foot wall. A platform on the wall's backside allowed the first girls over the top to lean back and pull up the others. The most difficult part was getting the last person up off the ground. It often involved draping someone down from the top, for that last person on the ground to use as a ladder.

In the Spider Web, a similar challenge, a rope web was strung from two poles. The team had to get everyone through the web to the other side without touching any of the strands. Most of them were just lifted horizontally and passed through like a log, usually accompanied by jokes and laughing. The first and last people were the most challenging.

I found it intriguing to watch how the patrols solved the challenges that sometimes had a twist and required clever thinking.

For example, the students gathered at a small pond, similar to the one under the ropes course. A tire tied to a tree limb hung at chest level over the center of the water. Three poles lay to the side with a hank of rope and a full bucket of water. The pond, the students were told, was a swamp full of crocodiles. They were given thirty minutes to move the whole team and the bucket of water from one side of the pond to the other. Anyone who fell or stepped into the water was "dead." They could only use the available equipment and soon learned that the poles were too short to reach the other side. At the end of the exercise, the patrol lost points if water spilled out of the bucket and if patrol members "died."

Another exercise involved cooking a raw egg with a few matches and a safety pin. Apparently it is not the custom in their families to poke a hole in an egg to prevent it from breaking while cooking. Some teams spent an inordinate amount of time figuring out why they had been given the safety pin.

Usually, the dominant students made the obvious suggestions. If the team tried them out without success, it was sometimes a girl who had seemed weaker in the physical challenges who was able to figure out the successful strategy. After that, the dynamics in the team shifted to a more balanced respect for everyone, each student with her own strength.

One afternoon, the assignment was for each patrol to create a play for presentation that night. Several resembled Rudyard Kipling's *Just So Stories for Little Children,* imitating the animals we saw on the plains. They all spoke. One was always wise. The students had great fun putting them together, usually much more fun than the actual presentation. And though they may not have recognized it, teamwork and leadership were involved in that activity as well.

While the girls were working on their plays, I joined four other instructors on a tour to one of the game parks. We saw most of the ungulates again, but were disappointed to miss the big cats and rhinos. It was hot and we decided they were napping.

On the way back, we picked up a hitchhiker, a young Masai man. He was wearing Western clothes and not the skimpy ochre robe I had seen on other Masai warriors. We stopped to pick up a bag of corn for the school. The order was not ready, so we all waited near a herd of goats. We chatted with a *mzee,* an old man, who'd been tippling. He compared *pombe,* homemade beer, to God. The younger Masai, who seemed rather worldly or at least wanted us to think of him that way, ignored him.

We loaded the corn in the dark. Then, the moment we had hoped for. We sped down the dirt road, headlights ablaze, and caught three cheetahs trotting along the road.

Monday night we celebrated with a wonderful bonfire, roasted corn, and singing. The next day, the students all left in high spirits. We instructors had time to complete our reports and enjoy the resort atmosphere.

When the course ended, I felt good about what I had accomplished and learned. I had climbed Kilimanjaro, an old dream come true. I validated that I needed to trust my own wisdom when working with a military-style leader like John, our uncommunicative boss. In teaching and leading the small patrols of girls through danger and cooperation, I had found the first kernels of leadership in myself.

Harriet

Reaching Gilman's Point at 18,640 feet on the rim of Mt. Kilimanjaro, the end point for most climbers. Harriet is on the left. Mt. Kilimanjaro is the tallest free-standing mountain in the world, its highest point on the rim, Uhuru Peak, at 19,340 feet.

CHAPTER TWELVE

End of the Fifth School Break

MONDAY, AUGUST 28, 1967

Dear Mom and Pop,

On Wednesday, one of the temporary OBMS instructors, Dave, drove Neila and me from the Outward Bound campus to Moshi and dropped us at Neila's house. Dave was supposed to stay with Carl Halpern, but Carl was not around, so we shuffled beds and he stayed with us.

Right now, I'm at the hostel in town because yet another Peace Corps person wasn't home to welcome me into her free digs. I've been bombing around town, gathering information about the athletics competition and doing errands.

Tomorrow, I move to the teacher training college. The athletes are staying there and it's near the stadium. They arrive by train tomorrow. I will be so glad to move because it is really hot here in town. Mwanza is never like this. Yesterday afternoon at the peak of the heat, I was plotting a route to my next destination and wondered if I could even make it. Heat and humidity do me in faster than anything. The sidewalks were scorching. The humidity made me so weak my legs felt like lead. I remembered a nearby bank and made a little detour to cool down in the air-conditioned lobby.

Harriet

WEDNESDAY, SEPTEMBER 6, 1967

Dear Pop, Carol, Mom,

I'm so happy that people's eyes pop when you mention I've climbed Mount Kilimanjaro. It really makes me feel that in two years I have accomplished something worthwhile.

My girls did not do as well as I had hoped in the national athletics competition. They arrived after the one-month vacation. The girls were hard to motivate before they left school and I'm sure they didn't do any training at home. Other competitors were from upper primary girls' schools where classes had been in session for the past two months. Obviously, they had been practicing hard. Oh, well. Still, the Mwanza team did remember something because they came in second, anyway, though individuals from the other schools did better.

However, after I heard about the trip the national team had on the way to the East African Games in Kisumu, Kenya, I'm very glad none of my girls were on that trip. The Tanzania team's private bus kept breaking down. It left Dar late Monday and got to Kisumu on Saturday, just in time for the competition.

Dar to Nairobi should only be a 10-hour trip. The girls spent all but one night in or near the bus, usually in the cold and rain. Needless to say, they didn't do very well. The great favorites from Rosary SS, our chief rival here in Mwanza, made the team, but they did not do as well as they should have, either. They were pretty arrogant when they competed here, but still didn't deserve such a bad trip. It would have been an honor for anyone who was actually chosen to compete, so I'm sorry none of the Mwanza girls made it for that reason. I wonder if Olympics' organizers know what goes into getting a team together in some countries.

I fear the enthusiasm among the old staff here at school is flagging. We all like this location, the students, and the other teachers. Generally, spirits are high, but no one is overactive. Our staff room is lively during breaks. Things get done, or they don't, as always. Now, we just don't get ulcers over things that get lost. Maybe that's how we should be.

Kathy S., Anita, and I, who did almost everything for Sister last term, have decided that this term she can do her work as headmistress. That's her job. We will teach. That is ours. We don't mention things that need to be done anymore because we always end up doing them. I do mention the things I do want to do, like putting together the teaching timetable. When I did it before, I arranged three free afternoons for myself. *Ho ho!*

I have traded Form III biology class for Form I physics-with-chemistry. I'm glad. I ran out of new things to teach the students in Form III. Re-teaching something isn't as fun as new stuff.

I hung the Ugandan bark cloth that I bought in town on the wall. It looks cool. Anita and I have lots of souvenirs all over the house. With all this exposure, I'll be ready to give it away by the time I get home.

I got a letter from a friend on where to stop and stay in Asia. At this point, I am thinking of stopping in Kabul, Afghanistan, and one or two cities in India,

Bangkok, Singapore, Fiji, and maybe some others. I'm still thinking about it.

One term to go. I just hope I can get through this term without more disruptions that take away from the teaching.

Harriet

CHAPTER THIRTEEN

Sixth School Term

Dear Pop, Mom, and Carol,

We shifted classes around, expecting three teachers would leave for National Service, but then the plans changed and they are still here and teaching, which is great for the rest of us. Right now, I'm only teaching 20 periods a week because I was supposed to teach the Form I physics-with-chemistry. A new British volunteer is coming who can take it.

Now that the national athletics competition is over, my team hasn't been practicing. No one else is doing any extra activities either. We won't until Sister gets them organized, which may be never. I try to teach and not let the disorganization get to me. It's tough.

Anita and I are down to 2 dogs and 3 1/2 cats. The half is one that hangs around but isn't ours. We can take the extra cats to the new city kennel that is opening soon. There are lots of stray dogs in the city. We almost lost a cat the other night. Anita and I were reading in the living room and the cats were outside. Then, the night exploded. A leopard jumped onto the porch and skidded across the slick surface. Cats scattered in all directions. Furry bodies everywhere. He would have caught a tasty dinner if he hadn't been off balance. I saw the whole thing and I'm glad he didn't get one of the cats. I wouldn't like to see one ripped to shreds even though we have too many.

The leopard was in no hurry to leave, so I got a really good look at him. He sat on the porch with his back to us, waiting for dinner to return. He was only 10 feet away (and a glass door between us). What a beautiful animal! Better luck next time, Mr. Leopard. The cats were smart enough to stay hidden.

The new teachers are getting settled. The two typing people are really nice, but one, a Canadian woman, is really unpleasant and might blossom into another troublesome Miss Jevons. She is in the Canadian External Aid program. They must have five years' experience before they are hired, then they get paid a regular (not volunteer) salary, plus 25% overseas pay, plus transportation of their whole house and car, and a trip to Greece after one year—plus, plus, plus! We'll see how she works out.

It's a hardship post here, lately. For the last week, we have been without water for several hours each day. It's unpredictable. The school doesn't have storage tanks to back up the pump by the lake. The workers are also repairing the electricity. It goes off without warning, often just at dinnertime. Exasperating! Anita and I have an electric stove, so we just pack up our dinner and traipse up to the gas stoves in her cookery room. Nice to know the right people.

Sister asked again today if I wouldn't extend my tour. The more she asks, the quicker I am to say no! If it weren't for the teaching, which is no longer a challenge, and the administration of the school, which is inadequate, I'd stay. The teachers are fun, though they are always leaving and being replaced. Most of the students are hard workers and easy to be around. This location is idyllic—nice house, view of the lake, gentle breezes. I guess I'd have to think of something useful to do or the ministry would kick me out. Details.

Tonight, Anita and I arranged to take some girls to see *The King and I,* a movie in town, but it was changed to *The Greatest Story Ever Told.* Not as great.

Harriet

MONDAY, SEPTEMBER 25, 1967

Dear Mom, Pop, and Carol,

Oh, nature is in full bloom. We have an ant colony by the power pole next to the house. In the evenings, the winged males emerge. A fabulous commotion of birds gathers in the waning light for a tasty meal. A mixed flock of at least fifteen species arrived last night, each bird trying to grab as many fat ants as possible.

I've sent photos of the birds that sit still. Two tiny birds are very colorful. The cute Red-cheeked Cordon-bleu has powder blue under parts, an unusual color for a bird, and a face with a bright red cheek patch (surprise!). The African Firefinch is a little bigger and has an olive back and wings, and brick red on its belly, throat, and face. The name is better than the color on the bird. It's a subdued red, but not fiery. Even a stunning Grey-headed Kingfisher was in the fray, so it doesn't only perch on a branch to look for food. Any *nummy* tidbit is welcome. The bird had a long red-orange beak and when it flew, its wings flashed a brilliant blue. There were lots more birds, but I didn't have much time to watch and look through the bird book, too. I took pictures with a borrowed 400 mm lens on a camera owned by a generous friend. He lent me the bird book, too.

Anita is a serious bridge player. She loves to host bridge games with the other aficionados. It's nice because people come and visit, but I'm not a player. I sew and work on my butterfly collection. I've mounted three sets of butterflies, now displayed on the wall. Quite well done if I do say so myself. The standard comment by visitors: "Have you seen the new film, *The Collector*?" What are they saying?

We are seeking another home for Sydney, our new dog. He is not home much and isn't much fun. This leaves only Simba, Anita's puppy. She is sweet and neurotic, very shy, and always sleeps under chairs. Unfortunately, she's getting too big for that and hasn't realized it yet. Last night, Anita got fed up with the dogs playing in the house and tried to confine them. Simba dove under a tiny stool, jumped up too quickly, and ran around the room with it stuck to her haunches. That didn't help her neuroses, but we were rolling on the floor laughing.

My Peace Corps insurance and my passport both expire the first of March. Unless a good job presents itself, I'll want to be in the U.S. by then. The cheapest way to arrange the trip is to get a through ticket and arrange stopovers, unlimited, and no penalty for changes. I told you it was a good deal! Carol, make your plans for meeting me and let me know what you decide.

Still no word about National Service positions for the Asians, so 17 staff averaged 21 teaching periods a week. Pretty easy.

Harriet

WEDNESDAY, OCTOBER 4, 1967

Dear All,

So glad my Kilimanjaro photos made it home all right. To answer your questions about the photos, the red jackets and most of the other equipment were supplied by the school—British army surplus.

I did wear my boots on the day we climbed to the top because I learned my lesson on the very first time we climbed up to the rock-climbing wall.

The Simpsons and Anita climbed Kilimanjaro after I did. They started the last day of their climb at 1 a.m. and they were very cold. Ken's feet actually froze. The water in the mountain stream was clear, sweet, and cold. We followed the stream from the bottom to one hour above the caves. We had to carry water up from there.

Today, Anita said she is renouncing her Canadian citizenship, frustrated and embarrassed by her fellow citizens. I don't think it will last. I'm afraid the Canadian External Aid people are not good representatives of her country. They're sent here as specialists, yet the jobs they do are the same as ours and we are volunteers. All seven Canadian reps in Mwanza act superior, plus they are bigoted, prejudiced, humorless, and conceited. They are all undereducated for their positions. They have absolutely no desire to learn about Tanzania or Tanzanians. After six months here, one of them asked me what TANU was (the only political party). The final blow was when Anita found out that one of the Canadian reps is going home for Christmas. She only arrived one month ago!

The electricity and water are back to normal. The dog is not. After Sydney left, Simba was lonesome. One night when we were away, she pulled everything she could up onto the sofa with her. My rain boots, the hammer, clippers. Now, Anita lets her sleep under her bed.

I'm sending a tape home of the girls singing. The first two songs were ones they sang for Saba Saba in the singing contest. The others are for Mrs. Berry's goodbye. I love how they harmonize.

Today, the new owner came for the big bookshelves that Kay sold before leaving. Our house is rapidly taking on the spare look of a volunteer's house. Glad I appreciated sharing with Kay. The only furniture that remains is really cheap stuff.

I heard a commotion outside the staff room during break yesterday. At the edge of the building a crowd of girls surrounded the new biology teacher. She seemed rather agitated and turned for the staff room as I approached. The girls were all looking at a five-foot-long monitor lizard. It was resting in the sun and eyeing us. We don't see many, so I was fascinated. The girls were giggling among themselves and I asked what was going on.

"Oh, Miss Dainsone," Dorah said, "she asked us about that lizard and we told her that it loves human milk and is deadly poisonous. It is not true, but we did not know how afraid she would become."

I had to laugh. As they joined me, the monitor stalked off, probably looking for a more peaceful place for his morning nap.

Anita says hello.

Harriet

SUNDAY, OCTOBER 8, 1967

Dear Al,

Happy birthday!

We took Mary and "Brim" Brimcome, a new couple, to Dancing Table Rock today. Brim works on a survey crew and brought some stereo aerial photos of the area. Really cool! Now I know why we kept getting lost on our runs. All the trails are so curvy; the bumps and outcroppings don't really have a logical pattern. I guess that is how it is with casual paths laid down by hungry cattle.

When we returned, the house was a total mess. Simba chewed everything she could: my rain boots, my chemistry "bible," and my insect collection board. She is now hiding in the most remote place she could find, under my bed. She never goes there. She is quivering, but she's just lonely now that she's the only dog.

There is a great hullabaloo because President Nyerere arrives soon for the TANU conference. He started on a walking tour several days ago to show support for the Arusha Declaration, which is TANU's Policy on Socialism and Self Reliance. It was a spontaneous decision. Nyerere is requiring his cabinet to accompany him. The photo in the paper shows him smiling and greeting people, but the ministers don't look so thrilled. He is thin and fit. All of them are overweight and out of shape. The first day they walked 12 miles and the next day, 22 miles. By the time he arrives in Mwanza, he will have walked all the way from Musoma, about 60 or 70 miles. Meanwhile, Who runs the country, I ask?

This morning, the girls were supposed to walk five miles to the regional headquarters to meet him and walk back to town with the entourage. After repeated post-ponements today, now he will arrive tomorrow morning. The plan is for one hundred girls from all the schools to walk the seven miles out from town to meet the president and walk back with him. Good luck. The students will find it difficult because they don't exercise much.

Sister asked me if I would go with them. I said no because I had a good idea of what will happen: We will be ready at 6:30 a.m. as planned, and the buses will be late. Then, we will amble to the meeting place, a pace I cannot bear. We will wait four or five hours and when we arrive back in town there will be no transportation back to school. Thanks, but I've played that game before. At this point, all I want to do is teach.

Of course, all this stuff means school will be chaos with the classes cancelled. What to do with the girls who stay here, which will be most of them?

Some of the new staff can go to see the president and walk. It will be exciting for them.

The Asians leave for National Service next Saturday, which means more work for the rest of us, not that we've been overworked. My replacement, Bronwyn, is supposed to arrive Tuesday, so I'll give her some of my classes and mentor her the way I was when I came.

Well, Anita and I finally got rid of the cats since the leopard did not do the job. After Grimalkin shit a huge pile of worms, we could delay no longer. We drowned them. Am I getting hardhearted? I just grit my teeth and do it. Too many unspayed animals around here! And they all seem to love our house.

Unfortunately, the hyenas haven't done their job either. The bodies are beginning to stink.

Harriet

MONDAY, OCTOBER 16, 1967

Dear Family,

What an exciting week! The TANU conference is in full swing in town. VIPs arrive every day. Nyere, along with Milton Obote, President of Uganda, and Kenneth Kaunda, President of Zambia, are the biggest names. According to a newspaper account, for some reason, Jomo Kenyatta, President of Kenya, turned back after starting the drive. Joseph Mobutu, President of the Democratic Republic of Congo, declined the invitation—probably due to political turmoil.

All of the Tanzanian parliament and TANU officials are here. Every extra bed in town is in use. The Israeli ambassador was listed to stay with the Brimcombes, but they got his political aide, instead. Kay and I drove in to town to gawk. The Mwanza Hotel has a line of flags along the front for the different countries. The international license plates on the parked cars indicate the celebrities in residence—very impressive. It's the most excitement we've had in a long time.

The Bwiru students have been practicing songs and dances for several weeks in honor of the visitors. They presented them last night after dinner and did a great job. Twenty of the older girls are helping in the convention hall where the speeches are made. I hope they get an earful. Who knows? Maybe some will become politicians. They need a lot of women! It's all men at the top.

Tomorrow, the delegates really get down to business, though I hear the conference is not well organized. They have a huge agenda. The Arusha Declaration laid out a lot of major changes. Now, they have to figure out how to make them happen. Changes include social equality, self-reliance, and economic cooperation with the other African states, along with *ujamaa* (family hood). If even some ideas work out, it will be progress.

With the Asian teachers away for National Service and Bronwyn marking exams, I teach 36 periods a week. *Arghhh!* Must be some kind of record, but I've taught it all before, so there isn't much prep.

I'm busy making plans for my trip home. My approximate arrival dates will be December 13 in Karachi, January 10 in Rangoon (Burma) and Bangkok, January 31 in Kuala Lumpur (Malaysia) and Singapore, February 14 in Brisbane, and my final stop, Hawaii, on March 1.

Anita envies me. She wants out!

Harriet

TUESDAY, NOVEMBER 7, 1967

Dear Carol and Mom,

Please get the American Express book that lists all their offices. Very tiny print, but handy. All the flights get to the cities I will be visiting late at night. I can pick out a hotel in my little book and show it to a taxi driver. Only the best are listed. Then, I can find a cheaper place the next day.

You can send mail to the American Express offices in Karachi, New Delhi, Calcutta, and Singapore. I'll pick it up when I arrive. In Thailand, send it to the Atlanta Hotel in Bangkok. In Brisbane, use Lennon's Hotel. I expect to be in the New Delhi-Kashmir area around Christmas, but don't send any presents. I won't be able to carry anything more with me. I'll only have my old army pack for stuff, plus my sleeping bag. I'm going to get really tired of the two skirts and three blouses I'm taking. I'll be the only one to know since I won't be seeing many people for any length of time, so it won't matter. Besides, I don't have any decent pants to take. We have to wear skirts for school and travel so I only have the one pair of ripped-off jean-shorts, which I'm leaving here.

Today, I finally picked up the wooden box of beautiful *m'ninga* wood that I ordered long ago to get the rest of my stuff home. It has such a mellow color, dark with some grain that I like. It is a chest 4' x 2' x 18", and the wood is 7/10 of an inch thick. The workmanship is not great, but I only paid 80 shillings, about $11.50, which is good because it is bigger than what the builder based the price on. I was almost driven to tears with his excuses and delays! Maybe he was hoping I'd give up, which I almost did. Anita bought a similar one at an auction for 50 shillings and it is much sturdier. "They just don't make them like they used to." Oh, well. It is here and almost packed.

We have the rest of this week to teach Form IV classes, then they take the Cambridge practicals in biology and physics-with-chemistry, and the written exams. Next week, we have four days of teaching, a day of exams, and then three more teaching days the following week. The end is in sight! Hooray!

Harriet

FRIDAY, NOVEMBER 24, 1967

Dear Pop, Carol and Mom,

Today is Mary Brimcombe's birthday. My *m'ninga* trunk has been shipped off for a boat ride home. I leave here next Thursday. Last Saturday, Anita and I hosted a "do" for the departing teachers; Steve, me, and a couple of others. I knew half of the people, the rest were friends of the new VSOs (Voluntary Service Overseas), Canadian volunteers like Anita. People brought food and Anita cooked some side dishes. I helped Anita grill dinner. The moon was full and we were lucky there was no rain. What a miracle! There was no dancing, not something I enjoy doing in public, so, I especially enjoyed it.

Yesterday, Steve Sterk hosted a Thanksgiving dinner potluck. I took potatoes and beans. Jake, a new Peace Corps Volunteer, cooked a delicious turkey. One man brought real grapes! I think they were imported from Greece. This Saturday, Cathy Baker is having another party, a "swingin' one," she says, so perhaps I won't stay so long since I'm not a "swinger." The next day, the girls are doing their goodbye singing and dancing for us. The final days will be full!

The rains have come. My poncho is again the envy of all who see it, even though I do get wet. The rain is so hard it goes right through umbrellas as a fine spray. The rivers that pour down our steps and down the gutters are amazing!

I've just made the world's only portable butterfly net out of a wire hanger and part of a broom handle. I'm all set to collect insects on my way back. I have a killing jar, a bit of chloroform, and a metal box with a hard foam bottom for the mounting process, and lots of the skinny pins. Customs had better not interfere.

Harriet

WEDNESDAY, NOVEMBER 29, 1967

Dear Mom, Carol, and Pop,

Well, school is over. I must say that most of the staff seem rather grouchy. I'm glad I'm leaving. The Cambridge exam was not overly difficult. The girls should have done all right. They gave a fine goodbye performance for us. One afternoon before their goodbye, I heard them laughing while practicing. I think they enjoyed the creation part more than the performance.

Carol, I'll write to you at the American Embassy in Tehran for you to pick up when you get there. Say "Hi "to the Thachers for me. [Nicholas G. Thacher, my father's cousin, was deputy chief of mission to Iran in 1967]

See you in Bangkok, Carol! And Anita says Byrd's Custard Powder is sold in Canada, so I won't bring any home. I think you have unjustly glorified it. When it is the only sweet treat, its taste seems unbeatable, but next to some good fatty ice cream, maybe not. *Num!* Fatty ice cream. I'm ready for some right now!

I must make some food for my train trip *tomorrow!*

Harriet

FRIDAY, DECEMBER 8, 1967

Dear Mom and Pop,

Everyone, friends and staff, came down to the train station to see Steve and me leave. It was most embarrassing because the train did not depart on time. Most all of them hung on to the bitter end when the train finally left. I'm sad to leave some good friends behind, but I am *ready* for my trip home. So much to see! So much to do!

Mwanza was cool when we left, but Dar is hot and humid. A few days have been nice, but yesterday, *whew!* All of my PC group stayed at the Salvation Army Hostel until yesterday for our debriefing. It's a huge place with lots of service people staying there, volunteers, missionaries, etc.

For meals, we all eat in an enormous dining hall with screens on the open sides and old, creaky benches. The food is served a course at a time. No matter where you sit, the staff always serves the right course even though people sit with friends who are half way through the meal. They keep track by the cutlery at your place. Each course has a knife and fork or spoon. If you refuse a course, they remove the utensils for that one and the next server knows what to put at your place. Clever.

I caught some nice butterflies. My killing/pinning and storage equipment worked very well.

The PCV conference was not taken too seriously although we have many final details to handle before we go our separate ways—forms, interviews, etc. Two days of saying things we all knew so a PC staff person from Ethiopia could write it down. It was fun to see everyone; some people I haven't seen since we first arrived. Most were happy in their schools, and we generally agreed we were a successful program. We exchanged notes on our next travels. Several people are going to India, but not as fast as I am. I may spend less time in Karachi and more in Rangoon. I'll see.

In town Monday, I saw one of my students. It turns out that the girls going to Moshi have been camping out in the railroad station since the train arrived from Mwanza on Saturday. The road to Moshi was washed out. No bus was available to take them around it. I talked to someone at the Ministry of Education about this and they promised to find beds for them if they didn't leave that day. I hope they do, but the girls are pretty resourceful.

My credit card has limited value. Peace Corps will reimburse me for the airline ticket home, but I have to pay for it here. I tried to pay for part of it with my credit card (American Express). I only needed to charge $210 out of $1,120 for the airfare, but East African Airways wouldn't accept it. They have to cable New York for approval. There is at least a 12- to14-hour wait for a reply. After numerous calls, I gave up and used some of my travelers' checks. I'll stick to just using the card to buy travelers checks because it's too much bother otherwise.

I had to cancel my morning flight to Nairobi due to the credit card problem and go this afternoon. I was able to make good use of the extra time. I took Steve's mother to the village museum. They have models built of all the different kinds of houses in Tanzania. Quite interesting.

I hope to get a letter in Nairobi, especially from Carol. I still want to leave there around the 13th.

Harriet

Dear Family,

Sorry I haven't written more while traveling. After I pick up my mail at the American Express office, I like to take your letters to my room and savor them in privacy. When I finally get a reply written, I have to find a post office, and stand in a long line to get a stamp.

I've been on the go ever since leaving Tanzania. Rather than returning home by the shortest route, I chose to travel to the east from to check out other countries I might like to revisit later. After what I've seen of India and Pakistan, they are not high on the list for returns, so that shortens the list. I tried to get a ticket to Burma, but Pan Am doesn't stop there because of the U.S. embargo. Carol and I are thinking of visiting Thailand, Malaysia, Australia, and New Zealand, along with some other possibilities.

After leaving Tanzania, I flew to Karachi, arriving around midnight. After an uncomfortable and expensive night at a tourist hotel, I found a cheaper place. Then I wandered around seeing sights until I needed a break. It doesn't take long. Maybe I am not open to what is in Pakistan after leaving my home of two years in Mwanza, Tanzania. Karachi seems so crowded and noisy. And so far, I haven't been dazzled by much, anyway.

At the Karachi bus station, the man at the information desk spoke good English, as most people do who deal with tourists, except for the "wannabe guides" who pestered me when I went near a tourist attraction. The bus station clerk told me that I should visit Thatta where there were some old tombs, and it's only a hundred kilometers [about 62 miles] east of Karachi. The bus reminded me of public transportation in Tanzania, crowded and old, so I felt right at home.

I was the only one who got off at Makli Hill outside of Thatta. At the bare crossroad, there was only a small café and a large house with a peaked roof across the empty street. After a cold night in the cavernous house, I visited the tombs. I only needed a few hours to see enough Arabic writing on stones and round-topped tombs to satisfy me. I was the only person looking at the tombs except for an old man who wanted to be my guide. He did not speak any English, and even though I shook my head, he kept beckoning me to follow him and pointing at things that probably have an interesting history.

It got very hot, so I walked back to the rest house. I'm sure the house was delightfully cool in the summer, but the nights were cold so the house was chilly even in the afternoon. I sat on the steps until I got hot and then moved into the shade—very pleasant. The café across the street offered six chicken dishes for my two dinners. That's it. Kinda funny, and it shows how resourceful the cook was since there were never many people eating there.

I returned to the United Hotel in Karachi and was pleased to see the toilet in my new room even had a toilet seat! And the room was warmer than the Thatta guesthouse, which seemed heavenly.

From Karachi, I took a quick flight to New Delhi where I stayed at the YWCA, assigned to a cold cubicle with a curtain for privacy in the dormitory for temporary guests. It was a long room with an arched opening to the outside, and no door. Greta, a nice German girl on a world tour, adopted me and we had good chats. I enjoyed her company since I sometimes feel as if I am in a bell jar, unable to actually talk to people. Pointing and smiling only goes so far. Swahili would not be useful, I fear. Greta was practicing her English and she was easy to understand.

Sunday, the two of us took the New Delhi city tour in English—very nice and just the right amount of sightseeing for me. Talking with Greta helped me realize why I feel so low. When I am around the really old buildings in this ancient city, it is clear that there has been great wealth in a few hands for a very long time. In Tanzania, with the colonialists have gone and the people are starting over with all things being relatively equal. The girls I taught are the hope for a better future. Here in India, I don't get that feeling of hope for a better life. The caste system is awful, and will be difficult to change, even though there are some attempts to do so.

I have not seen a good public park yet with trees and grass where I can relax. The parks I have visited have sad peacocks strutting around with no tail feathers because someone plucked them to make a bit of cash. Sad, but it makes sense in this place. There is trash everywhere, only adding to my dislike of cities. Even Dar es Salaam was not like this.

Of course, I had to see the Taj Mahal in Agra, about a two-hour train ride from New Delhi. I may never come this way again, so I didn't want to miss out on this unique architecture that Indians consider their "crown jewel" of Muslim art. My hopes were high and the building was magnificent, but after seeing the Taj, I have to admit that it was not as impressive as I expected—except for all the inlaid work. While looking at all of it, I just kept thinking, What a chore. I have to wonder if the workers who built it got paid and how that emperor had so much money, anyway, to spend on his third wife! It is such an opulent edifice while so many still live in hovels and starve. Once again I was reminded of the contrasts between India and Tanzania where no one will be building anything like the Taj Mahal anytime soon. I guess I took my conversation with Greta with me to Agra.

After a one-night stay in Agra, I took a four-hour bus ride to another tourist site, Jaipur, known as "The Pink City." It is certainly pink with most buildings painted a red sandstone color. I wasn't too impressed, but I guess I'm just not into buildings. However, I did enjoy the hot shower at the hotel where I stayed, and the weather for this semi-arid region was quite mild.

It will be Christmas soon. No intense shopping in the cities since there are so few Christians here and Christmas is not a big holiday. Much as I hate the hype at home, I wouldn't mind hearing *Sleigh Bells Ring,* or maybe *Winter Wonderland,* both totally inappropriate for here, but not for me.

Carol might have already left Oregon on her way to meet me by the time you get this letter. I am still planning to be in Bangkok by January 21 and I'm looking forward to seeing her again. Travelling with her will change my experience and I'm ready for a change.

We should be home in March, which will complete an around the world trip for both of us. Wow! I hope we'll have lots of good slides to show you when we get there. In the meantime, I wonder what I'll find to do until Carol arrives—I am hoping for something more engaging than what I've found so far.

Harriet

Looking Back on the Peace Corps Experience

In Tanzania, I took on responsibilities and met challenges that drew on all my mental and physical resources, often pushing beyond what I thought possible. I developed confidence in my own judgment and a more discerning attitude toward authority.

After two years experience a the Bwiru Girls' School, I felt I could have done an adequate job as headmistress since I was doing much of that work in addition to my teaching load. I declined to extend my stay—I had taught every course twice, which felt like enough. I was young. Tanzania seemed to be moving forward. My country was in the painful throes of the Civil Rights Movement. The Vietnam War was heating up. I had no set plans for my future and the world waited. It was time to leave Bwiru to discover what was in store for me in the United States.

Those years in Tanzania were historic not only for me but for the country. It was a privilege to experience the joys and tensions of nation building at the ground level. Two years before my arrival, Tanganyika had united with Zanzibar to form the new country of Tanzania. Mwalimu (teacher) Julius Nyerere became the first president, a brilliant and peace-loving man doing his best to guide his people through the pitfalls of independence. To President Nyerere's great dismay, human weaknesses and a crippling drought destroyed his dreams and idealistic plans.

I returned to Tanzania in 2008 as a birder, and found the country finally shaking off some of the woes brought by the settlement schemes and corruption. Seranero in the Serengeti, where my mother and sister and I stayed in upscale huts, is now a nice lodge built around rock outcropping with rock hyraxes making their homes under the stairs and giraffes wandering by. The older lodge on the ridge above the Ngorongoro Crater felt about the same as when we stayed there, which is a shame after 40 years. Many of the rooms were still being refurbished after years of neglect. I think this was the saddest moment of the tour for me, a stark reminder of how far Tanzania had declined since I left. The positive side is that the country is recovering.

The tour did not go as far west as Mwanza. The only town where we lingered was Arusha, located at the base of Mount Kilimanjaro. I had passed through Arusha several times when I was in the Peace Corps. I wondered if any of the older women my age would recognize me, but none did.

My friends and Canadian volunteer colleagues, Kathy Simpson and Anita Foley, stayed on at the Bwiru Girls' School a few more terms. They reported that Sister Jacques Marie turned out to be an excellent headmistress and remained at Bwiru for several more years before retiring. After our string of headmistresses, that must have been a relief to everyone.

Anita became a medical doctor and practiced in rural Guysborough, Nova Scotia until her retirement. Kathy and Ken Simpson lived and taught in several countries before returning to Canada. Most of my Peace Corps friends returned home to continue teaching in the United States.

Kay returned home the long way past South Africa. She and Steve lived in England while waiting to be accepted into graduate school, and then moved to the Boston area for their continued studies and teaching. Shortly after the birth of their son, Steve was tragically killed by lightning. Soon thereafter, Kay took a college job in Iowa where she eventually remarried, and where she still lives.

What moved me forward years ago was the belief that I was training tomorrow's teachers. As I was doing research for this book, I discovered that there still are Peace Corps Volunteers at Bwiru.

My life metaphor comes from my experience at sea, watching a tiny tugboat push around an enormous ship. Patience and persistence win out in the end if you don't quit. I learned after leaving Tanzania that I can't save the world, but it is important to do what I can. After 10 years in the women's funding movement, and 23 with a progressive foundation, I know it works.

—Harriet Denison
JANUARY 2014

223

HARRIET DENISON

About the Author

After Harriet Denison returned home from her Peace Corps work in Africa, volunteering remained a part of her life. While living in Vancouver, British Columbia, she earned a Master's Degree in Human Resource Development and consulted with nonprofit boards to increase their effectiveness. She also served on the local and national boards of several nonprofits.

Denison permanently returned to her hometown, Portland, Oregon, in 1986. Her mother, Margaret Denison, had been the manager of the Oregon portion of The Ralph L. Smith Foundation in Oregon (RLS) for thirty-five years. When Harriet returned, Margaret transferred responsibility of the family foundation's day-to-day activities to her. Denison served as the foundation's unpaid staff for more than twenty years.

As part of her philanthropic activities, Denison volunteered in the early formation of the Women's Funding Movement, which focused on women's leadership and causes. She founded the Women's Foundation of Oregon in 1989, which supported women's groups until its dissolution in 1996. Denison also served on the board of the National Network of Women's Funds, renamed Women's Funding Network (WFN) during Denison's tenure. For two years, she served as board chair of WFN, and retired from that board in 1999.

Today, WFN is the largest international philanthropic network of women's funds dedicated to improving the lives of women and girls worldwide.

During those ten years of national philanthropy, Denison learned hard-earned lessons about organizing for change and leading a diverse population toward a common goal. Denison's work with women's funds informed her local philanthropy as well. Under her guidance, the mission of the RLS Foundation in Oregon evolved *to promote equity, justice, and sustainability.* The foundation supported organizations that addressed the root causes of social, economic, and environmental problems. Denison and her family tried to effect institutional change at the policy level and worked to more equitably balance the power in society between those who have the least and those who have the most.

In line with the foundation's values, Oregon's RLS Foundation gave its assets to three sister-organizations in 2008; McKenzie River Gathering Foundation, Western States Center, and CAPACES Leadership Institute. These three grassroots organizations share common values, and the public boards are comprised of people from the communities served by Oregon's RLS Foundation.

Denison took her first writing course in 1995 at a Flight of the Mind Writing Workshop for Women in Oregon. Since then, she has participated in ongoing women's writing groups. Her first book, *Travels with Turtle, From Oregon to Nova Scotia and Return,* was published in 2003.

In addition to her writing projects, Denison hikes, paddles dragon boats along Portland's Willamette River, and does yoga and tai chi regularly. Denison can tie a bowline with one hand; a skill she says would come in handy "if I were hanging onto a ledge with the other hand." Add to those skills, weaving and family genealogy.

Denison also sings in Portland's Threshold Choir. In groups of two or three, the singers visit the bedsides of ill and dying individuals to bring them ease and comfort at the thresholds of living and dying. The choir's vision is to offer their gift of song by being a calm and focused presence with gentle voices, simple songs, and sincere kindness—elements that can be soothing and reassuring to the recipients, and to their families and caregivers.

Throughout her life, Denison has pursued her passion for travel—both nationally and internationally. Starting with Oregon, she has visited 254 incorporated cities and towns, and has photos to prove it. She has also visited and spent at least one night in every state in the United States.

Internationally, Denison's travels have taken her from Antarctica to Madagascar, and New Guinea to Zanzibar. Her world adventures have involved serving and studying in numerous countries, as well as serious birdwatching, sailing, bicycling, hiking, and more. She returns from her travels with astute observations, humorous stories, and exciting adventures to share. Simply, Denison leads an impassioned life in whatever she pursues, and generously shares her experiences.

Learn more about Harriet Denison's travels at her website: www.travelswithharriet.org

Made in the USA
Lexington, KY
01 June 2014